THE ARSONIST IN THE OFFICE

Fireproofing Your Life Against Toxic Coworkers, Bosses, Employees, and Cultures

THE ARSONIST IN THE OFFICE

*Fireproofing Your Life Against Toxic Coworkers,
Bosses, Employees, and Cultures*

Pete Havel

Clovercroft Publishing

The Arsonist in the Office: Fireproofing Your Life Against Toxic Coworkers, Bosses, Employees, and Cultures

Published by Clovercroft Publishing, Franklin, Tennessee

Copy Edit by Gail Fallen

Cover Design by Nellie Sanchez

Interior Design by Suzanne Lawing

Printed in the United States of America

978-1-948484-66-4

FOR THE RECORD

This is a work of fiction. Names, characters, businesses, places, sequences of events, locales, and incidents are either the products of the author's imagination or used in a fictitious manner. Any resemblance to actual persons, living or dead, or actual events is purely coincidental.

Additionally, I'm not a lawyer or a psychoanalyst and am not providing a diagnosis of any character depicted in this book nor providing legal advice of any kind.

DEDICATION

To Janie, thank you for your patience
during this labor of love.

To Reagan, thank you for who you are, your great
book ideas, and amazing editing skills! And, yes, I'm
finally done with "the book" for a while!

To my sisters Mary and Anne, my mom, the rest of my
family and all my friends, thank you for your support, the
laughs you provide, and some of the great material.

I love you all.

INTRODUCTION

You may be one rogue employee away from burning down your organization and your culture.

Or one wrong move from seeing your career go up in flames.

I know. It happened to me. Do you wonder if you could be next? Or, maybe it will be your reputation that's destroyed. Or your company's culture and productivity attacked.

All it takes is encountering the arsonist—the destructive employee with the mindset and the tools to light things up and burn you down and a culture that lets them thrive.

Toxic, destructive people—arsonists, as I call them—when empowered or ignored, can do irreparable damage. The arsonist can be the boss's best friend, a man or a woman, a relative, or a longtime trusted leader. They can lurk in the shadows or do their dirty work in broad daylight.

Have you worked with an arsonist or in a toxic environment? You probably have or know someone that has. They create havoc, cause great employees to run for the exits, and hurt productivity, just to name a few problems.

But incredibly, in too many organizations, arsonists are thriving. Through acts of omission or commission, too many leaders in organizations tolerate horrible behavior if the employee is somewhat productive . . . or litigious . . . or black-mailing someone . . . or if they can punt the employee down the hall or into another department.

When they blink or dodge instead of take action, they are putting the gas can in the arsonist's hands.

Millions of people every day live in unnecessarily stress-ful and dysfunctional conditions because of toxic coworkers and cultures, while decision-makers watch from the sidelines or protect themselves at the expense of their organizations. When that happens, all hell may break loose.

What can be done? How can leaders prevent fires from breaking out before their organization is at risk? How can employees—whether facing a destructive coworker or a cor-rosive culture—protect themselves in an atmosphere that eats away at common sense, kindness, and careers?

When equipped with the right tools, anyone can identify the arsonists and protect themselves and their organizations.

This book offers tools and tactics that everyone—from employers to employees; Fortune 500 to Mom and Pop small businesses; and members of PTAs, churches, and chambers of commerce— can use to protect themselves and their organi-zations against toxic people and cultures that destroy careers, morale, productivity, reputations, and financial success.

I have spent my career working in some of the toughest environments imaginable: working as a political operative in everything from local to presidential campaigns, serving as a lobbyist for some of the most powerful organizations in the country, and helping crisis-riddled companies pull back from the brink of disaster. I understand, like few people can, the world of big egos, major negotiations, and tough personalities.

In my career, I had handled everything. And everyone. I felt bulletproof until I ran into the one situation I was utterly unprepared for, that is. I was hired to work with the employee called "the arsonist."

Hired into the most toxic workplace imaginable and forced to partner with an employee so toxic and combustible that managers said they were afraid to manage her, much less fire her, I witnessed an organization paralyzed by decisions that led them to keep an employee who burned down everything in sight. Instead of putting out the fire and taking away the matches, they chose to sweep the arsonist's ashes under the rug time after time. When an organization protects an arsonist, at some point the script flips. Management, in an effort to do damage control, actually begins to work for the arsonist.

What followed for me was void of reason or explanation. Good people became consumed by fear and operated in self-interest and self-indulgence. Absolute power corrupts absolutely and an absolute toxic culture does, too. With the wrong moves at the top or the wrong culture, what happened to me can happen to you. And it can happen to your organization and its culture.

Determined that no one should face the challenges I faced without an ally and a game plan, I have written this book to give employers and employees the tools and information needed to survive and operate in in a toxic environment—and to transform it. Leaders everywhere need a gut check and a new resolve to face the toughest, most uncomfortable issue in the workplace: dealing with the arsonists. I interviewed over 300 business leaders regarding their thoughts on dealing with personnel matters. Many are doing things right, but many admit they're limping along to simply get through another day.

I believe we can do better—by our employees, our shareholders, and the values of our organizations.

Whether you work in a toxic workplace, with a toxic coworker, or you want to protect a great culture within your organization, this book will give you tangible takeaways that will help you fireproof your culture from the arsonists in the office. I will also tell you what to look for when deciding your next career move to avoid walking into the job that may rock your career to its core.

It will help anyone who is frustrated, without hope, and wondering what to do in a workplace that more closely resembles a war zone. It may be an employee working with a toxic coworker or boss or the executive of a company who realizes that their decision to look the other way at bad behavior from one or a few key employees has jeopardized the company's future. I will provide information, answers, hope, and the motivation necessary to take bold action to make changes for the better.

What's separates this book from the pack? You can find plenty of great books on the toxic workplace written from a psychologist's perspective or from a human resources professional's view. Those books are wonderful, and I have learned something from all of them.

My perspective is different. I was in the belly of the beast in a toxic workplace and lived to tell about it. I've dodged the missiles, suffered a few attacks, and seen the fear in the eyes of managers who had simply given up. What I learned, you need to know. What I witnessed, you need to understand.

I pull from my deep experience in political battles, crisis communications, and a wealth of information I learned firsthand about toxic organizations and difficult people to inform you of how to react—things you will never know until you're in the middle of the fires of an arsonist's inferno. In my career, I've been the manager and the employee, the hunter and the hunted, the candidate and the person doing opposition research, the person who has coached corporate leaders through a crisis, and the person who's been in the middle of one. When you are out of answers and feeling confusion or desperation on how to respond to tough workplace situations,

I am confident that this book will be a trusted companion on your bookshelf.

Many business books tell their story through parables. You will get that here, too. However, my parable is my own fictionalized story—based on overwhelmingly heavy doses of hard truth—and it's not your average parable. It's got some kick. And my truths will hit you right between the eyes with some things you need to know about situations that happen every day. But few have written a book about them.

This book is also a call to action. Leaders can create cultures and their inattention to problems can destroy cultures. The inability to deal seriously with destructive people and ignore cultural problems is a sickness and a symptom of other illnesses within the leadership ranks. If you can't deal with removing a destructive employee or correcting a poisoned culture, what else are you ignoring at your own peril?

Companies have let things get out of hand—whether on the assembly line or in the C-suite, the executive level of organizations. In some countries, it's becoming incredibly difficult to terminate an employee. In government, there are agencies making the disastrous decision to promote toxic employees to make it easier to get them out of their department.

No one deserves to be abused, handed combat pay to deal with the organization's problem children and told to like it, or forced to clean up the problems that decision-makers have willfully chosen to ignore. We deserve better and will all be more prosperous if we step up and say no to the arsonists.

It's time for a movement that people on every step of the organizational ladder can embrace and help lead. It's time to protect our productivity, our employees, and our cultures. It's time to fireproof all the important things we value most.

Finally, though my story deals with an arsonist that

happened to be a woman, arsonists are from both genders, all races, every political stripe, and all faiths. It's why virtually everyone I speak to has a story about an arsonist that they have known.

Are you ready to join the fireproofing movement? Are you ready to extinguish the arsonist in your office?

CONTENTS

Chapter One

FIRED UP

I entered my new employer's doors for the first time that Monday morning with unbridled excitement. Energized, motivated, and ready to run through walls, I felt like this was a dream job. Within hours of setting foot inside the company, however, I started to wonder what kind of crazy dream this was.

The timing of taking this job was perfect, as the company where I had been working previously was being shut down by the retiring owner. Because of that, I needed to find a job quickly, and I found one. "The firm," as it was known, was one of the fastest-growing government relations companies in the country. They snatched me up and hired me to cover a huge portfolio that stretched from coast to coast.

Now, if you're not familiar with what government relations means, that means we lobby.

Which makes me a lobbyist.

The Cambridge English Dictionary defines lobbyists as

"those who try to persuade politicians to do something."[1] The rest of society that doesn't write dictionaries defines lobbyists as "dregs of society," "thieves," "cancers," and "con artists"—all extremely harsh (we have feelings, too!) and highly inaccurate, but I'm writing this book to protect you from toxic people, not launch a branding campaign for lobbyists.

Lobbying has been my chosen field, though, to be honest, the lobbying life chose me. I'm a persuader, a storyteller, a relationship builder, and a heck of a good listener. I know how to read people—or at least I *had* been pretty successful at reading people up to this point in life.

I can imagine some readers recoiling at taking advice from a lobbyist, and you're not alone. Gallup's 2017 survey of Americans' ratings of honesty and ethical standards placed lobbyists below car salesmen and even members of Congress. In fact, lobbyists placed dead last out of all professions.[2] I hope all of you in other jobs are grateful for those of us in lobbying for keeping your professions out of the basement!

But that's OK. I can only control what I can. I recall the way I was once described by a legislator to his group of government reform minded constituents in the room: "Pete's a lobbyist, but he's honest." The crowd looked puzzled, as I don't think they knew such a thing existed and certainly had never seen a real live honest lobbyist in their lives. I felt a little guilty, as I don't think the crowd trusted him as much after complimenting me!

I have represented the business community in Washington, DC, and across the US by working for some of the top trade associations in the country—powerhouse organizations with which you are probably familiar. I've also run some political campaigns and been an executive in strategic communications companies that help organizations build their brands, communicate a message, and survive during a crisis. I've even led a chamber of commerce.

Because I grew up in a small-business family, I have enjoyed helping build an economic environment where jobs are created and employees and employers benefit. I've worked with governors, members of Congress, senators, presidential candidates, cabinet secretaries, CEOs, and the great political minds that make so much of the horse trading happen.

Lobbying requires cooperation, sociability, listening, and persuasion. You need to stand your ground, but you also have to be flexible. It's hard work and long, irregular hours, but it doesn't really require a lot of heavy lifting. A lot of the work is done in fun, low-key meetings over coffee, lunch, or at political fundraisers. As for the rest? It's done under brutal conditions that sometimes put you in front of some very angry people.

It takes many skills, but the most important is the ability to work with just about anyone. Understanding and tolerating the vast range of egos, experiences, and opinions is a must. No matter what you think personally, you have to be able to hold a conversation with the right, the left, and everyone in between. Your adversary one minute might be your strongest ally the next. I've put together some of the most successful—and occasionally, the most unusual—coalitions imaginable because I'm not afraid to talk with someone who may not agree with me. It's that ability to get along with everyone and navigate through a wide range of personalities that often got me job offers.

It's also these skills that have allowed me to maintain life-long friendships with dozens of people I have worked with over the years.

The interview process for my job at the firm had been pretty standard stuff. Now that I was hired, I would report to Suzy, my soon-to-be supervisor; and Cecil, the self-proclaimed "Sultan of the C-suite." As Suzy explained it, my role had been created out of responsibilities held by a current employee, Hazel. I would take most of her responsibilities, and Hazel would hang onto the rest. No matter the reasons for the change, I knew it was going to be a little awkward.

I'll make things work, I thought. *How bad can it be?*

From the outside, there were no particular warning signs. In fact, it looked to be a great opportunity—great salary, huge levels of responsibility, excellent benefits, a high profile, and many perks. And Suzy and Cecil could not stop raving about the Emeritus Partner program, a retirement benefits program they spoke of in almost spiritual, nearly evangelistic terms.

The only concern at all was that the duo had used, on multiple occasions, the phrase "special challenges" to describe what I would face in the job. I had asked a few times what those were, but Suzy brushed it off.

In fact, I pressed Suzy seriously in one of the interviews and, looking back, should have known then and there that something was wrong. Why? Her reply wasn't a reply. It was a dodge. "Every job has its challenges, Pete." That's all she said. And that, my dear reader, is the old political press-conference trick of speaking to a question but not answering it.

But I thought that if anything was a truly serious problem, they'd tell me. Where I got that idea, I'll never know. I should have realized that if they were telling me about the problem, they hadn't acted to solve it.

Typically, a new hire expects piles of new information to read through, maybe an orientation, and a few meetings with key people. You get your name badge, your office, and a summary of benefits. Direct-deposit information is taken.

You switch over your health insurance to the company plan and hear about the "top of the list" types of priorities you're expected to focus on in your first thirty, sixty, and ninety days. In some way or another, we've all done this drill.

But while I got those things, I also got something else entirely: the creeps. As I made my way around the offices and met my new colleagues, their comments to me were more appropriate for someone whose dog had just died or was facing a terminal illness than a new employee. Sure, I was handed some business cards and hearty welcomes, but mostly I got cryptic warnings, oversized eye rolls, and comments left dangling without explanation. Condolences, but no clues as to why.

- "I'm praying for you." I believe in the power of prayer, but they had just met me and seemed to have something in mind.

- "Hang in there, buddy." I got this one when I'd only been on the job a matter of hours.

- "If you ever need to get stuff off your chest, just call me." Just your average friendly pre-emptive offer of counseling.

- "Watch your back." Recruiting-poster worthy!

- "There are lots of jobs out there if this one doesn't work out." I had worked about twelve hours in total when I heard that.

My new coworkers were friendly—strangely friendly. They behaved as though they had known me all their lives and seemed to love me like a brother. That was nice but odd. When they spoke, they did so in hushed tones. Some pulled me into corners and looked both ways before speaking. That was . . . unusual.

Comments continued to mount. I thought about what I was getting myself into. Was I confident in my ability to perform the work? Absolutely. Did I feel good about the organization? I had no reason not to be. The pay was good, and the opportunity to excel was there, but something was nagging at me.

It was the unnamed, vague, "special challenges."

A few days in, I walked into the break room for the first time and bought a soda from the vending machine. As I took my first sip, an older gentleman in a sweater-vest strode up to me and offered up his hand to shake mine.

"You must be Pete. I'm Ted," he said. "Welcome to the firm. Can I ask you a question? What have they told you about your job?"

"I'll be handling lots of projects, but I'll definitely be working on the National Spelunking Association account, helping the Fish Noodling Alliance, and a few others." I said.

Ted's face curled up in a knot—in confusion or annoyance, I wasn't sure which—and I certainly didn't know why. "You're missing my point, Pete. Exactly what did they tell you about your job and who you're working with?" Ted said.

"Well, I report to Suzy, and then I'm working with Hazel. I'll be helping clients all over the country," I said.

About the time I was about to ask Ted a follow-up question of my own, Cecil popped his head into the break room, and Ted raced from the room with a parting, "I better go," like he had a date with a stomach virus.

"Pete, do you have a few minutes?" Cecil said.

"Anytime the boss wants to talk to me, my schedule is free," I said, smiling. "Let me grab a notebook and a pen, and I'll come down to your office." I raced down to my desk, grabbed what I needed, and headed down to Cecil's office.

I knocked on Cecil's door, and he waved me in. He was a

tall, stately, elegant man, his jet-black hair masking his age. He'd enjoyed a long and storied career and was known for his ability to survive in any situation. "Pete, welcome," he said, shaking my hand warmly and thoroughly with the unusual two-handed handshake used only by politicians and preachers. He gestured for me to sit down in the chair directly across from him. "How are you enjoying things at our not-so-little firm so far?"

"Well," I said, "it's been a great start."

He nodded. "Good, good. That's what I like to hear."

Then I added, "There's a lot to learn, but I'm hitting the ground running." I talked about some of the experience I brought to the position just in case he needed to hear it again. However, I left out the unusual chatter from my new coworkers.

That was accidentally wise because, in doing so, I gave time for him to deliver the mother of all on-boarding sessions.

Cecil paused for a moment and looked at me as though he were sizing up the green on the 18th hole of the Masters, analyzing the angles, so he could tap in that winning putt. He was studying me. Then he put a finger to his lips to signal his request for silence and sought my nod of agreement. After a few seconds, he stood up, walked over to the door, and closed it with great deliberation. He trudged back to his chair in a slow lumbering way, as though the weight of the world rested upon his shoulders. He sat down, leaned back, steepled his fingers, and met my eyes. He was a showman and looked ready to put on a show.

"Just so we understand each other," he said slowly in a syrupy drawl sharpened in the streets of Bunker, Missouri, "everything I am going to say is highly, highly confidential."

"Of course," I said.

He wasn't done with the disclaimers. "If anyone asks, I will deny we ever spoke. Am I making myself clear?"

Apparently, this meeting was not about how to join Cecil's fantasy football league.

I swallowed hard. "Yes, I understand." What did he suspect I would do? Start live-tweeting from his office?

Once the blood oaths were out of the way, Cecil got focused. "We need to discuss Miss Hazel," he said.

I just found the special challenges, I thought.

What followed was a mix of apologies, confessions, fables, contortions, and confusion, while detailing record-setting achievements in the world of human resources complaint filings.

"You're probably not going to like me much," he continued, "but you need to know some things. Better late than never and no better time than the present. And frankly, I'm not sure how long you will want to be here. But let me start with some data points."

In my world of government relations, data points were results of opinion polls, appropriations details, metrics, and research into complex policy problems, not my boss opining about how long I would want to stay in this job (making him, by the way, the second person in just a few days who had gone down that road). What followed was less data point and more horror movie trailer.

"Hazel," he said, "is, she, uh . . ." He parachuted out of his comment mid-sentence and appeared to be desperately reaching for the right word. "Hazel is interesting. She's very entangled here . . . and accusatory. The entanglements have been factored into how we deal with her. Previous leadership had, well, *entangled* to create a mess of a situation. As a result, this organization is sensitive—very, very sensitive—in dealing with her."

"What's an entanglement?" I asked, dipping into my mental thesaurus as I wondered what definition of that word I hadn't heard before.

He guffawed. "Let's just say it's an entanglement. You figure it out! I'm not drawing you a diagram, boy!"

Gulp.

Cecil nodded, intuitively sensing my building curiosity—and growing nausea. "Things have happened internally that I would prefer remain internal. Internal should stay internal. The internal cannot become external. The past is the past. The future is the future."

And with that rhetorical fortune cookie, I knew why Cecil had thrived for so long in politics. He had just been folksy, thorough, compelling—but hadn't said a darn thing.

"Those entanglements and other special circumstances have caused me great distress and significant effort to clean up. I don't like cleaning up my own messes, much less somebody else's," he continued. "I have changed the reporting lines, so Hazel no longer reports to me."

"Here, look," he said. He reached into his desk and began feeling around for a colorful, laminated masterpiece of an organizational chart. Once he found it, he pulled it out like a boy who had reached into his stocking on Christmas morning and found a baseball autographed by his favorite team. Resplendent with squares and rectangles, lines and dashes, titles and acronyms, Cecil held it with the pride most people reserve for their firstborn. "You see this line here? It ain't here anymore!" he excitedly said, beside himself with glee.

Cecil beamed momentarily but then leaped toward the serious. He removed his glasses and rubbed the bridge of his nose and eyes. In a second, he suddenly looked like a man who had not slept in months.

"Hazel's like a bottle of tequila—strong, powerful, and able to put you on the floor if you mess with it. She's filed probably at least a dozen, maybe fifteen, sexual harassment complaints and even more than that number of hostile-workplace environment complaints. She gives 'em out like candy. She mounts them on her wall like some people do deer heads and diplomas. They're all baloney. She doesn't just abuse the system. She is this system! She knows where the bodies are buried because she's buried them! I don't want these bodies floating up to the surface in a heavy rain, if you know what I mean."

I picked my jaw up off the floor and gathered myself.

I began doing the math. Division, calculus, and spreadsheets filled my mind.

Thirty complaints divided by X number of years = perpetual, overwhelming grievance!

I started to think if I knew of anyone who had filed even one human resources complaint in a previous job against anyone, much less thirty! I couldn't think of anyone.

I cleared my throat and asked Cecil the question I just couldn't resist. "Cecil, are you worried about Hazel accusing you of something?"

Cecil paused and looked at me with great seriousness and intensity. He got up, straightened his tie, walked over to his door to grab his suit coat, placed the coat on, and sat back down. This was incredible. Theatrics were on display in his every utterance. It was mesmerizing.

"Well, you should be worried!" he said. "I'll tell you facts. No fiction here, boy! You will never see me meeting with her alone. Not if I can help it. You better do the same.

"Be careful about what she tells you," he continued. "Information is currency around here, and she'll give you funny money. What's the old saying, 'Trust, but verify'? I'd verify every word she says, writes, or winks because that little meteorite's not happy you're here. Sorry to tell you this now, but it's a little unprofessional to bring up delicacies like this in an interview, and you might not have taken the job."

MIGHT not have? And I was pretty sure he meant delicate situations, not delicacies.

Had I been hired to be a lobbyist or a crash-test dummy? Food taster or javelin catcher? Decoy or lab rat? Who and what was I up against? With almost perfect timing, Cecil was about to tell me.

"Pete, let me explain Hazel," Cecil said, assuming I really needed more explanation. "Have you heard the story about the volunteer fire department that had a rash of fires start up in their community?"

I hadn't, and shook my head no.

I won't belabor the details too much, but as Cecil explained it; it was the volunteer firefighters who were setting the fires. "Some lit 'em for kicks, others lit 'em because they knew they would not get extra equipment if they didn't have enough fires in their county, and others just liked watching things burn. A few burned things down because they didn't like the people who owned certain properties, and some others liked being called into city hall and called heroes. Some were even helping their buddies by torching buildings for insurance money," he said, looking me square in the eye. "All that? That's Hazel."

"You just described an arsonist," I said, mentally dry-heaving.

Cecil chuckled. "Yeah, she's kind of the arsonist in the office, and now she's your arsonist, too! Careful she doesn't set you on fire!"

Looking back, I don't think Cecil realized how right he was. The arsonists we tend to think of burn down buildings, but the arsonist he referred to burns down companies, people, careers, and cultures. We know the motives of arsonists in the criminal sense. Arsonists in the office have similar motives. They just have different tools and targets.

- Arsonists sometimes cover up evidence of other bad acts. Arsonists in the office are motivated to act out to distract from their own failures.

- Arsonists can have a super-hero complex. Office arsonists like to be seen putting out fires, even though they started them!

- Arsonists often act for financial gain. In the office, how much trouble is created because people want to leapfrog over others to get a promotion, cut corners on ethics to pump up their numbers to trigger a bonus or a raise, or attack coworkers they view as competitors?

- Arsonists act out of revenge. Created out of jealousy or badly formed views of justice and entitlement, arsonists in the office burn down other people around them to right the wrongs they see.

- Arsonists do things for attention. Arsonists in the office torch things for recognition. They are adrenaline junkies who love to light the match and see sparks fly!

I had heard of people like this before but, unknowingly, Cecil had crystallized this type of employee to perfection (and gave me a great title for a book).

I had no idea how to respond and sat dumbfounded, while Cecil had energy to burn and things to say.

"Be vigilant! Be dynamic! Not so hard, huh, boy?" he said, speaking in a confusing mix of Winston Churchill and Andy Griffith-like exhortations.

His words were almost offensive. *If this is so easy, maybe Hazel can camp out in your office for a few days, Cecil!*

"Cecil, if Hazel is making up charges like you say, why is she still here? You just called her an arsonist. If somebody files a complaint because they were harassed, more power to them. They should get justice. But someone who is making things up to target people? What am I supposed to do with this, and why wasn't she fired for making false complaints?"

"Let me be succulent, we decided it was, as we called it, 'cheaper to keep her,'" said Cecil. "Do you know how much hell she'd raise from outside the organization if we fired her? The legal costs? The PR firms I'd need to hire? The leaks? She'd burn this place down in every way but fire if we got rid of her. Her mind doesn't work like other people's minds do. She's ruthless. But I got your back. Don't you worry!"

Cheaper to keep her? I thought. *Have you guys checked the batteries on your calculator? And, for all things that are good and holy, I think you mean succinct!*

"I keep my friends close and my enemies closer," Cecil said, "so Hazel and I will be sharing blankets and making brownies until one of us leaves," he said, creating a visual that nearly blinded me with its audaciously uncomfortable description. "The tricky part for you is that you two need to get along, and she'd like to choke you to death. You took a lot of her job. The good news is that it sounds like you get along with everybody. Buddy, you'll do great."

"Any questions before we wrap up, Pete?" he asked. I had plenty, but I learned I don't speak well when I'm in shock.

"I now understand what everyone else has been warning me about," I said.

"People shouldn't be gossiping. I don't tolerate gossip!" he said, this after discussing entanglements and arson for the last half hour. "Oh, and one quick thing," Cecil added. "Your notebook. Can I see your notes?"

I handed over my notepad that barely had more than a scribble on it. He scanned it, saw the vast nothingness of my remembrances, and handed it back. "No notes when we have guy talk, OK?" he said.

I headed back to my office to sort through what had just happened, unsure if I felt dirty or whiplashed. Cecil had warned me, but his warning was like telling me about recent shark attacks right after pushing me into the water.

And what was with taking notes from me like a prison guard confiscating contraband on visitors' day?

I had worked hard to develop and maintain a good reputation throughout my life in high-profile jobs, so I can tell you I was horrified about what I had just heard. Being accused of something like sexual harassment is a stain, one that doesn't come out. It follows people everywhere and taints everything people have done in their careers. I had not signed up for this.

I didn't sleep well that night or for a long time.

But Cecil's wasn't the last warning of my onboarding process.

On deck: Suzy for round two.

Just days after I met with Cecil, Suzy said she wanted to have a "little meeting" later that day. The quaintness of the description made me envision scones and tea. We planned it for shortly after lunch.

When I entered the office, Suzy was on the phone chatting with a friend. Her workspace could be best described as a file cabinet with windows. Papers everywhere. Folders piled in ways that mocked their intended use as an organizational tool. Suzy was an informational packrat—three-ring binders filled the room with what looked to be information collected since the beginning of time. An affable woman with a frenetic and scattered delivery, she had the strange gift and curse of sounding both keenly interested in what someone was telling her while also nervously looking around like she had forgotten to turn off the stove at home. Her blazing red hair was always arranged in a tight bun, her eyes alive and expressive, and her past work as a full-time free spirit and part-time yoga instructor was clearly evidenced by the ever-present smell of burning incense and the occasional chant you might hear within earshot of her office at the right time of day. While diminutive, her omnipresence of activity built a large footprint.

Finally, she ended the call.

"Sit, sit! Okey, dokey, where were we?" she said, clearly forgetting that we were precisely nowhere. I was just looking at her.

"So let's talk about Hazel," she said. She was back on track.

"I had a feeling. Should I close the door?" As if there was any doubt.

"Yes, please."

And with that, the floodgates opened.

"You had a good conversation with Cecil?" I nodded, but good was a bit of a stretch. "I guess I haven't been totally open with you," she said.

"Really, how so?" I said, in my best shocked-sounding voice.

She took a deep breath and folded her hands on the desk. "Hazel. Terrifies. Me."

"How come?" I asked, hoping that I was acting sufficiently surprised.

"I've been Hazel's victim in the past, and I'm scared of what she might do now that you're here. Obviously, you know Cecil made me her manager!"

I measured my next words and took a deep breath. "He mentioned that right before he called her an arsonist."

"Cecil loves that story. He's so descriptive," she said. "But I actually think she's like a terrorist because she is very stealthy in how she fights. I mean it as a compliment. She doesn't kill people. She's sneaky. She is quite fascinating."

Cecil called her interesting and an arsonist. Suzy called her fascinating and a terrorist. The mix of terms sounded like we were discussing either science experiments, national security interests, or both.

"I have a few friends at Centcom who can bring in an anti-terrorist Special Forces unit," I joked. Mostly.

Suzy's eyes grew wide and concerned. "We can't do that."

Apparently, anti-terrorist raids were prohibited by corporate policy, as was an understanding of sarcasm.

"She's come after me before, too, so don't feel sorry for yourself. I have no idea what to do with all of this, Pete."

And we hold these truths to be self-evident . . .

Suzy's comment worried me, and the indecision that followed didn't change that. In the Super Bowl of managerial challenges, Suzy had just been pulled out of the stands and put on the field to play quarterback—with ballet shoes on and a baseball rulebook. I provided some quick and easy management lessons I had learned over the years and asked a few questions to help her think through her challenge—no, make that *my* challenge. I could see why Cecil didn't want to have Hazel report to him, but dump her on Suzy? That idea would not age well.

"You need to monitor what Hazel does," I said. "If she causes problems, she needs to know there are consequences."

"That could be a problem," she said.

"When there are problems, you document them and deal

with them. Another company I worked for described dealing with the actions of problem employees as PICs or NICs and managed them accordingly. Positive, immediate, and certain consequences if someone did something right and turned their behavior around. Negative, immediate, and certain consequences if they didn't. We do have company processes, right?" I said. This was Management 101 type of stuff.

She stiffened up.

"Right, Suzy?

"Suzy?"

She nodded with a lack of resolution that indicated that she was nodding externally, but not internally. Suzy's body language reminded me of those hostage videos where the captive talks about how well they're being treated. And of discussions with a good friend of mine whose wife is from Bulgaria. In Bulgaria, nodding means no and shaking your head means yes.

"Sort of. But I don't know whether they apply. This is a strange situation. We are kind of writing our own rules here," she said.

Truer words had never been spoken, and traditional management protocols had been shredded—figuratively or maybe literally. You don't write rules on the fly. Not if you want to maintain order.

I thought I'd change the subject and pivot to a topic of major interest to me: the false complaints and the incoming fire that Cecil had warned me about. "Cecil told me that Hazel has filed thirty or so false complaints, maybe more, against people around the firm. What are you going to do if she starts making frivolous accusations while you're managing her?" I said.

"We'll figure it all out. We have time. But you really ought to be careful. Things could get a little crazy," Suzy said.

That wasn't an answer, and I wasn't sure who was "we."

"We're paying you well, though. Think of it as combat pay since you're fighting terrorism, or arson, or whatever we'll call it," she said with a laugh.

And that wasn't an answer, either.

"Oh, and Pete, obviously don't trust Hazel. She'll make you look foolish," she said.

"I've heard," I said. *After you hired me, that is.*

Now I had a question for Suzy. "How am I supposed to partner with someone that you say is out to get me?"

"You're a smart guy, Pete. You'll figure it out. It's why we hired you." she said—just like Cecil had.

I wasn't sure about the "figure it out" part, and upon the realization that I had stumbled into this mess, I started to question the "smart guy" analysis. With nothing else to add to her comments, I thought I would do something that people always say is good to do in meetings: be positive and constructive.

"Any ideas on how to make this situation better, Suzy?" Kevlar vest? Witness protection program? Admittedly, I had asked for ideas.

"I think that you and Hazel need to go to lunch," she said.

"Lunch?" I asked, my voice cracking, seemingly auditioning for third-grade boys choir.

"Think of it as an icebreaker," she pitched. "It could be just what you two need."

(Historical note: the *Titanic* broke ice, too.)

She raced through a flurry of self-congratulatory comments about the brilliance of this luncheon idea. "Oh, this will be great! I'm so excited," she said, literally clapping and beaming as she delivered the words.

"You have to do this. It'll be great. Think of it as a peace offering!" she said.

Like Neville Chamberlain?

Let me ask you as a reader: What do you do when your supervisor in a new job directly tells you that you should do something? Hazel had not threatened with me a complaint since I started the job a few days earlier, which was a plus. *How bad could it possibly be?* a part of me thought, while the rest of me was violently opposed and wanting to revolt.

"OK, we'll go to lunch," I said, and I slowly walked back to my still nearly empty office. I closed the door, took a deep breath, and did a mental inventory of my first few days. I compiled it neatly in my mind:

- Arsonist

- No, *terrorist*

- Combat pay

- Trust, but don't trust

- Boss says she has no ideas

- Brownies baking

- Blanket cuddling

- Thirty complaints

- Cheaper to keep her?

- Special Forces raid canceled

And I'm about to go to lunch with a flamethrower. *Now* what do I do?

Chapter Two

SIGNS OF A TOXIC WORKPLACE

Is your workplace toxic? Do you know what it means? What it looks like?

In my case, when I joined the firm, I didn't know what a toxic workplace was. I equated it with whiny people who couldn't cope. I'm not somebody who enjoys psychological exploration—I'd rather watch football. I hadn't thought about it much, but I thought it largely meant working for a jerk. Most of my previous bosses had been great, so I really didn't have much insight. Nor did I know how fortunate I had been in the past.

The vibe from my first few days had been strange, bordering on the surreal, but I thought things would blow over. They often do in life and usually had for me. The firm had an obviously difficult and maybe rogue employee, but they acknowledged it. That seemed like a good thing. If they know they have a problem and are acknowledging it, they'll respond accordingly if their problem becomes my problem, right? As I learned, not necessarily.

Let's define what a toxic workplace is. Generally speaking, a toxic workplace is one wherein drama, chaos, and dysfunction trump common sense, where established ethical standards and reason are overtaken by survival instincts and self-interest. It's a land where common decency and civility are ignored in lieu of expedient abusive behavior.

You'll notice my practical definition here is the absence or the elimination of good, accepted societal norms and the insertion of poisonous qualities. Without good values underpinning a culture, toxic values can quickly fill the void.

Toxic workplaces are created when decision-makers either behave badly themselves or look the other way and do not address bad behavior from others. Toxic employees are of course responsible individually for their behavior, but management has a responsibility to step in if the behavior affects others. Management has sole responsibility for workplace culture and is responsible for dealing with bad behavior. Management shapes cultures—both through action and inaction.

Spotting a toxic workplace is a lot like how US Supreme Court Justice Potter Stewart identified obscenity and pornography in the 1964 case *Jacobellis v. Ohio*. In explaining why material in question was not obscene, Potter said, "I know it [pornography] when I see it . . ."[1]

Identifying and analyzing toxicity is similar. In the words of Dr. Bennett Tepper, chair of the Department of Management and Human Resources at Fisher College of Business, toxicity is the "the sustained display of hostile verbal and nonverbal behavior, excluding physical contact."[2] Much like people, a workplace can have a bad day, so the occasional or the inadvertent bad act isn't necessarily the sign of bad things. Weeks, months, years, or decades of bad behavior, however? Likely toxic.

Wondering about your office or your organization? Check out my "Toxic Top 20"—the most obvious signs of a toxic workplace.

1. People don't voice opinions out of fear of reprisal. This inhibits innovation, restricts creativity, and sends discussion underground.

2. Bad behavior is ignored, explained, and even defended. If they don't want to address an issue, they ignore it or even normalize it.

3. Personal space (lack of boundaries) invasion, and employee intimidation are the norm. Once the culture starts to roll downhill, things really start to snowball.

4. Problem solvers frequently leave the company to "seek other opportunities." They leave or are forced out when they voice concerns. Good people bail first.

5. Culture equals a poster in the breakroom. That's it. But hey, they checked that box. And the worst part is that a lot of managers think that poster really means they have established a culture.

6. Cutting, personal, hurtful barbs and teasing are commonplace. Things get personal quickly if a culture lacks standards. It is delivered like a joke, but it feels like an insult to the recipient.

7. Blistering emails fly. The internet is forever and the life of nastygrams is, too.

8. Employee humiliation is common and often used right

out in the open in meetings and group emails.

9. Processes and policies are ignored in place of pulling things out of thin air to match the circumstance.

10. Insults are in; constructive criticism is out. Evaluations and helpful corrective opportunities morph into run-ins with a crazy ex.

11. The "walking dead" roam the hallways. The less powerful and out of favor become intentionally nameless and faceless to their managers.

12. Those affected by policies are often the last to know about changes to them.

13. Control masquerades as management. "Under my Thumb" by the Rolling Stones plays softly in the background.

14. Employee feedback is ignored or shunned. Whether it's due to egos, distrust, or a complete lack of understanding of rank-and-file employees, employees are conditioned to only labor, not be part of a team.

15. Gossip is in; dialogue's out. The cultural destroyers in the organization are free to say whatever they want without recrimination. But here is the strange thing. Sometimes, depending on how bad the culture is and who is driving the toxicity, gossip may actually be more accurate than the official company line.

16. Management pits employees against one another. Monday morning leadership meetings devolve into cockfighting rings.

17. Turf wars, power plays, and survival trump productivity and excellence. The bottom line is that no one is

thinking about the bottom line.

18. Secrecy is a superpower. Useful information that could benefit everyone—especially the interests of the organization—becomes part of a game of "keep away."

19. Ethics are seen as a roadblock to getting things done. Doing things the right way becomes inconvenient.

20. Sleeplessness, ulcers, high blood pressure and heavy drinking become common. People literally become sick of their jobs.

Do any of these sound familiar?

In any job, you might see an action from time to time that looks like one of the Toxic Top 20. If you do, it doesn't mean a workplace is toxic. It may just mean that someone or a group of people are having an uncharacteristically bad day. But if you see many of these behaviors regularly? You have a problem.

In my experience at the firm over time, I counted a solidly consistent seventeen toxic behaviors I witnessed at least weekly. That's not only toxic; that's a burn and bury your clothes, EPA comes to put a fence around it, bulldozes it, and tells future generations to never go near it for fear of contamination, Chernobyl-level of toxic!

For employers and managers, think of what occurs when employees are afraid to speak up. In sales meetings, how many new ideas are never mentioned because of fear of being slapped down or embarrassed? How many employees are hurt because the culture teaches them not to speak up if they see problems?

How many good employees leave because they simply walk away in frustration? How many toxic landmines are buried around your company that will only be found when someone steps on them?

Read over the Toxic Top 20 list and see how many apply to your organization. If the answer is more than a few, management needs to take steps now to clean up the culture and investigate who and what is driving it.

For managers and rank-and-file employees or anyone else reading this, let me turn this survey around and ask you a really uncomfortable question. How many of the Toxic Top 20 apply to *you*? If you're part of the problem, identify it, admit it, own it, and change course.

Speaking of courses, it's time for the first course: lunch with Hazel.

Chapter Three

THE LUNCH

I agreed to go to lunch. I don't know what I was thinking either.

Going to lunch with Hazel was outrageously, mind-bogglingly, spectacularly stupid. But my supervisor said to do it, and I did.

The night before the lunch, I sat in my big leather chair in my home office, turning it over and over in my mind. I was a one-man debate competition. My confidence versus my gut feelings.

I kept thinking, It's lunch; how bad can it be? I've eaten lunch thousands of times without a problem. No Heimlich maneuver, no salmonella, and certainly no charge of sexual harassment. I can handle this. What can she possibly do? It's one darn lunch.

On some levels, I thought I could handle Hazel. Before taking this job, I had been shouted at by hecklers in the middle of speeches, been forced to have security consultants investigate my meeting locations for threats, had microphones shoved in my face by confrontational reporters, had organized walkouts from my speeches, been smacked over the head with political signs by drunken political activists, and survived conversations with angry constituents who were balancing on the razor's edge of fury. I had moderated debates and built some of the most complicated coalitions imaginable. No fear here!

My skin was thick, and my level of confidence was high—as it turned out, irrationally and incorrectly high.

But then I'd think, *Thirty complaints. Arsonist. Terrorist. Buried Bodies . . .* and lose every bit of certainty I had.

And as far as concerns about a sexual harassment charge, I convinced myself I had things completely under control because I had thought of precautions, including

1. We'd drive in separate cars.

2. We would have lunch in a large, open restaurant. In my mind, that meant plenty of witnesses. I wanted room for a marching band to be able to come through the place.

3. No chitchat. No personal conversations. All business.

Problem solved, right? Ha!

Lunch was scheduled for Uncle Cheung's, a popular Chinese restaurant in the area with a great lunchtime buffet. If nothing else, Hazel and I at least shared a fondness for Chinese food.

I arrived first and made a special request: a table in the middle of the room. The hostess signaled something in her native tongue to a colleague, and I was led to the table by a charming waitress with a happy smile. She seated me, and I awaited Hazel's arrival.

A few minutes later, Hazel entered the restaurant. I felt a cold sweat emerge.

Five feet eleven, with long brown hair and a tan that was

unusual for any time of year, much less winter, her eyes were large, probing—almost searing, and set close together. Her sturdy frame was adorned in normal business attire.

Hazel was a family name according to some, but others were left to wonder about its true origin. Hurricane Hazel, one of the deadliest hurricanes in history when it reached land in 1954, is famous for her ferocity, her breadth, and the unusual, pattern-breaking norms that wrought carnage all the way from Haiti to Toronto. Hazel's destruction was so notable that the name "Hazel" has been retired from all future use in naming of North American hurricanes.[1]

Was that a coincidence or history warning me?

As she approached the table, I rose to my feet and shook her hand. "Thanks for coming, Hazel," I said.

"Thank you for inviting me," she replied, giving me a head-to-toe look as we shook hands. Her baby-girl lilt contrasted sharply with her grown-up wardrobe.

As I sat down, I was puzzled by the strangely neutral expression on her face. I couldn't quite read it. I was focused on self-defense, given Cecil's and Suzy's comments, but I felt like I was being scanned. Not looked at, but looked over. Like a bull at a stock show.

Our waitress came and said she heard we had a special occasion. "Anniversary?" she asked.

"No! Wrong table!" I blurted out, with a bit more intensity than was likely necessary. "We work together," I quickly said to the waitress. "I'll do the buffet!" With speed rarely seen in a land-based mammal, I moved toward the food with Hazel trailing behind.

We picked up plates and proceeded to move through the line. I was in the lead, and Hazel was behind me as we selected items.

I'd pick pork-fried rice. And then she'd pick pork-fried rice. I'd choose Mongolian beef. And then she'd scoop some.

I would scoop out Kung Pao chicken; she'd do the same.

I would skip past five items to get pan-fried dumplings and, well, you get the picture.

By the end of the fifty-item buffet line, she had selected the exact same foods as I had, in identical portions. Was this a subconscious quirk or was it intentional? I didn't know which but headed back to the table.

The conversation hit a lull from the outset, so I thought I would fill the void. "So, how are you?" I said, clapping my hands together, hoping that would prompt me to say something useful.

"Great! Any problems so far?" she said.

"No, none at all," I said, wondering what the shelf life would be on that answer. "I do want to ask some questions and discuss some things to help get me up to speed in the next few weeks."

"Anything you want. We'll have fun together," she said.

Oh, no we won't, I thought. But I did need some information from her.

As we ate, we moved through my checklist at a good pace.

Hazel was cooperative and helpful at first, but then her train of thought began to go off the track—just as most train wrecks begin. Elaborate answers turned into short responses, which turned into one-word comments, and then into nods.

And then into . . . well, read on.

As I got to one of the last things on my list, Hazel interrupted.

"Let's change focus. We've talked about what you want. Now here's something I want to know. What have they told you about me?" she said with a half-smile and half—I have no idea what.

Cue the organ music.

Dun-dun-dun!

My breath caught in my throat. Hazel's was an understandable question given the chatter within the organization. However, I wasn't touching it with a ten-foot pole.

I liberated a bite of pan-fried dumplings from my plate as I stalled and misdirected. "Well, Hazel, I have heard good things and I . . . You know, you really have decorated your office well."

I looked up, and her eyes were locked on me, set on stun. It was an uncomfortably long stare. It was one of those stares where you aren't sure if a person is looking at you or through you. If I had been the sun during an eclipse, Hazel would be blind.

The stare continued. Before I could answer, I learned that all the Hazel hype wasn't just talk. It was right in front of me—in the flesh.

With all the precision of a heart surgeon, she expertly reached up to her blouse and unbuttoned a button. And another. The shirt parted slightly, revealing more than a glimpse of her cleavage. Not all of it—we were in a restaurant after all—but enough to know it was there. Her eyes glanced downward to her chest for several seconds and then up at me—a ritual that repeated itself a few more times. I was shocked. But was I really? In horror movies, are you really surprised that the killer is behind the door? Or surprised that the Hallmark Christmas movie has a happy ending because the frustrated female florist falls in the love with the sad widower? My utterly confused eyes darted anywhere they could to avoid the action.

My mind flashed to survival mode. Sorry, shouldn't have said flashed.

Check, please! I internally shouted.

I was simultaneously having the mother of all thought bubble discussions:

Q: *Did this just happen?*
A: Dude, look across the table. No, don't!

Q: *Why?*
A: The only thing better than thirty complaints against people is thirty-one.

Q: *Is this some kind of joke?*
A: Not a joke. Not a drill. This is a live artillery exercise.

Q: *Did anyone else just see this?*
A: I hope not. Or maybe I want a witness. No, I don't even want to see this!

Q: *Should I talk to someone about this?*
A: It may not matter. I may be rendered mute for the rest of my life!

I looked anywhere but in Hazel's direction—ceiling, floor, plates, shoes, my own shirt, customers at surrounding tables, you name it. I thought about baseball, future appointments, long division, war and peace, gas prices, and generally anything else I could pull into my consciousness.

Finally, Hazel re-buttoned with the nonchalance and ease of an automotive technician slamming down the hood after doing an oil change. She picked up her fork and returned to her food and the conversation like we had been talking about the weather.

I waved to the waitress to bring the check, but it was no longer just a check. It represented my last chance at freedom!

"Hazel, this has been great. I need to get back to the office. Have to run!"

Literally.

I bolted for the door and can't remember if I paid. Now that I think about it, I may owe them money. I only remember getting in my car and staring at the steering wheel. When I finally made it back to work, I closed the door and just decompressed—like an astronaut returning from space.

I sat and wondered what the heck had just happened and what would be the fallout from this craziness. Truth was on my side, but who would decide who was telling the truth if Hazel made a complaint against me? As Cecil had described things, Hazel didn't even need to have a conversation with someone to file a complaint against them. When—if ever—would I want to bring this up? I was embarrassed for even being on the planet for what had just occurred, much less at the table.

Just as I regained my composure, I heard a knock at my door. "Come in," I said.

Suzy popped her head in. "So, how was lunch?"

"My coworker just unbuttoned her top" was seconds away from coming out, but I held back.

"Lunch was . . . informative," I instead said with careful deliberation.

This was the first of dozens of times when I found myself conflicted about whether to ignore Hazel's madness or bring it out into the daylight with other people. I stewed on this issue for a while—the last thing I wanted to do was discuss this matter, but the second to last thing I wanted to do was get torched by Hazel. What do I *do*?

I had no idea where to begin. If there was a playbook, I had never read it. There's no twelve-step program for survivors. And I much better understood Suzy's utter confusion about how to manage Hazel.

As a reader, I know what you're thinking: Surely, this is as weird as it gets, right?

Nope.

Chapter Four

HOT TAKES ON SEXUAL HARASSMENT AND THE BATTLE OF THE SEXES IN THE #METOO ERA

When it comes to sexual harassment in the workplace, the issue is out of control because of three groups of people: harassers; those who look the other way, minimize or excuse harassment; and false accusers.

Let me say at the outset that any harassing workplace predator needs to be dealt with swiftly and summarily, assuming the facts are there! Jump through the right hoops and get rid of them.

I had never thought much about protecting myself against a sexual harassment charge, but once I joined the firm and especially after the lunch Hazel and I "enjoyed," I could not stop thinking about it.

Hazel wasn't a sniper. She was a carpet bomber. Thirty or more complaints. You'd have thought she was winning a free meal for every five complaints with the trajectory and speed with which she filed. Though the Kung Pao Cleavage adventure was absurd, I didn't want to take any chances. I knew that any comment or action—or nothing at all—could be and would be twisted. That was even before I found out how the firm dealt with frivolous charges (spoiler alert: they didn't).

If either of the following are true, (1) harassment is ignored and harassers are marginalized, or (2) false accusers are given free rein to launch accusations, you have the conditions for a free for all to break out.

There's no better way to land on the front pages these days than to get caught up in a corporate sexual harassment scandal. It can take down a person or a company and, in some cases, it should.

The #MeToo era started because Hollywood, Wall Street, and corporate America looked the other way when they heard about bad behavior. I support every woman who has been victimized by someone who ruined their career or preyed upon them. Because of those who stepped forward and talked about their horrible experiences, many companies have changed the way they think about harassment and thankfully so. It was time for some significant recalibration.

But just like tuning a few isolated keys in a badly out-of-tune piano does not make beautiful music and aligning only part of your car's suspension does not make the car handle better, solving only half the problem of sexual harassment and male-female interaction in the workplace doesn't fix things.

We need to fix sexual harassment in the workplace. To do that, we need the grown-ups in the room and ask the extreme voices to step aside.

Before you decide this chapter is only applicable to men learning lessons, consider the following: The demographics of sexual harassment claims are changing fast. According to the Equal Employment Opportunity Commission's document "What You Should Know: EEOC Leads the Way in Preventing Workplace Harassment," almost 20 percent of sexual harassment complaints filed with the EEOC in 2017 were filed by men. That's up from 7.5 percent in 1991 and 16 percent in 2011.[1] As time goes on, the percentage of women in management roles will grow. So, what I'm discussing in this chapter is relevant to everyone—not just men. And for every woman and man who is harassed in the workplace, we need to get it right. In a generation, women might be facing similar concerns to what men have today.

If you are being harassed, defend yourself. But be careful. Before speaking up, fully understand how your organization operates, so you do not become a victim twice. It's imperative that all of us understand our terrain. Pay special attention to Chapter 19 on "Smoke Detectors and Whistleblowers."

Now on to even stickier issues. For many men, the greatest fear in a workplace from a reputational standpoint is being falsely accused of sexual harassment (Notice I said "falsely." If someone sexually harasses a coworker or subordinate, they should have consequences for their actions and face the repercussions).

What is sexual harassment? What happens and what should you do if you're accused of harassment? How do you protect yourself from being accused?

Let's begin with what sexual harassment is. The EEOC defines workplace sexual harassment as "unwelcome sexual advances, requests for sexual favors, and other verbal or physical conduct of a sexual nature. It constitutes sexual harassment when this conduct explicitly or implicitly affects an individual's employment, unreasonably interferes with an individual's work performance, or creates an intimidating, hostile, or offensive work environment."[2]

A sexual harassment accusation requires an investigation, which will likely be led by your HR department, the company's legal counsel, or an outside consultant.

If you are the subject of a sexual harassment complaint, you must cooperate, not obstruct or delay. Stonewalling can get you fired, and the investigation will continue either way. The old saying "If you're not at the table, you're on the menu" applies here. So does "He who represents himself in court has a fool for a client."

Talk with an employment attorney with employee-side experience and, depending on the seriousness of the matter, retain them for as long as you think you need them. A phone call may cost you a little money, but it's chump change compared to the cost of losing your job, rebuilding your reputation, and filling in and explaining the gaping hole in your resume.

But talking to an attorney does not mean walking into the office and announcing you have "lawyered up."

Employment law attorney Dustin Paschal of the Texas-based Simon Paschal law firm, representing employers and employees, counsels a measured approach when you involve legal counsel. On that issue, Paschal said,

> Informing your employer that you have an attorney could portray you as a danger to your employer from a legal and risk perspective (i.e., you are getting ready to sue them and simply are gathering the information and evidence you need). Since complaints that have nothing to do with a legally protected category (i.e.,

race, religion, etc.) are not protected complaints, your employer could terminate you if they fear you following the news that you have hired an attorney. Assuming your employer does not terminate you, notification that you have hired an attorney can escalate the situation and sometimes inhibit your employer's efforts at investigating and resolving the situation. If you feel that you need an attorney, your best approach is to keep your attorney's counsel to yourself and use him/her as a sounding board and point of advice. But do not inform your employer about him or her. Your lawyer should only appear when legal action is needed.

Additionally, while unionized employees may have the potential for assistance for investigations involving them, non-union employees traditionally do not have a right to be represented in internal investigations. Paschal said the following on the subject:

> While an attorney certainly can provide advice and counsel, at least under federal law, a non-unionized employee of a private company has no right to demand representation during workplace investigations, interviews, discipline sessions, or counseling events. This means that you as the employee cannot demand that your lawyer be present in the workplace as your advocate.

To clear your name in an investigation, you need to speak on the record. You may need to provide a list of witnesses who will tell your side of the story and vouch for you.

Stay away from the person who accused you. Your organization will likely demand it, but regardless of what direction you get, avoid all contact.

If you are accused, know that companies can't make issues

"go away" other than by addressing the complaint that has been filed. Sometimes, organizations remove the accused for reasons other than what's on paper. They can terminate accused employees for some other reason, demote them, or make life so incredibly uncomfortable for them that they leave. It's literally making the problem—guilty or not—go away.

How can you avoid ever being accused of sexual harassment? After all, credibility takes a lifetime to earn and only a second to lose.

Here are a few ways—both for men and women—to hopefully avoid a sexual harassment complaint.

- Avoid jokes, stories, or pictures that have anything to do with sex acts or body parts. It can be difficult to know if you're crossing the line, so avoid the line completely.

- Recognize people for their work, not their appearance. "Nice work!" is good. "Nice _____ (fill in the body part)"? Not good.

- When traveling with colleagues, do not hold meetings with coworkers in private rooms, the hot tub, or anywhere else that you don't want to explain later.

- Keep doors open in all one-on-one meetings with all genders and, to potentially avoid charges of sexism, never, as a rule, have one-on-one meetings with anyone. Many elected officials and business leaders don't meet with anyone alone. There are plenty of good reasons for that policy, and avoiding allegations against you is one of them.

- Limit social contact with colleagues when alcohol is present. Drinking with co-workers, while common, is often generally asking for trouble. Do you want to be sitting in an investigation trying to detail how many drinks you had when an offending incident occurred? Usually, if you're explaining, you're losing.

- Don't date anyone in your company. This sounds extreme, but hey, this is a book about avoiding problems. But if you ignore this advice, remember a single "no" is your stop sign. Don't push it. A second or third request could be seen as harassment and increasingly is written into organizational policies on dating. And "no" doesn't even have to be an actual "no" to violate some organization's policies. "I can't tonight" or "I'm busy" is a hard "no" to companies like Facebook and Google, both of which have written detailed relationship manuals for the workplace. If you want to play with fire and date a colleague, you both should have a game plan in place from the very beginning. Read your employee handbook about whether you need to disclose the relationship and everything else you need to know.

- Never date subordinates. Full stop. Just don't. Too many things can—and do—go wrong.

- Understand your company's policies. For example, many companies don't explicitly prohibit telling dirty jokes, pinching someone's behind, or having relations with your assistant. Their guidelines are more of a behavioral road map, an overview. What those policies usually say is that you can't do things that are unwanted, cause someone offense, or cause any reasonable person to be offended.

Let's not sugarcoat what happens to people who get fired for sexual harassment. Not surprisingly, it's a stigma. Here are some of the things that you can anticipate:

- Immediate termination so your company can avoid a

lawsuit against itself from the accuser. As mentioned earlier, this can be for petty, unrelated matters.

- Poor references or no references for future hiring. The phrase "not eligible for rehire" is often what's stated over the telephone. Other HR managers can read between those lines. (It is possible to negotiate for a neutral reference in the severance agreement, but even then you're in trouble.)

- Impossibility of answering the question "Why did you leave your last job?" in a way that ends well.

- Humiliation at having to explain to family and friends what has happened.

Losing your reputation can happen instantly. News travels fast, but salacious news moves even faster. Jobs come and go, but LinkedIn, Twitter, and Facebook are forever.

Avoiding sexual harassment issues is a combination of common sense, emotional intelligence, and not putting yourself in situations that can be avoided.

Organizations should know there is serious legal and financial jeopardy for not enforcing harassment policies or picking and choosing who or what gets enforced. Get this right! Follow your procedures every time or prepare to be sued at some point in the future for treating some victims or some of the accused differently than others.

Companies dealing with harassment complaints should be swift, complete, correct, and ruthlessly fair. Take politics, friendships, and emotions out of the equation. Remove the problem, no matter where it's found to be and no matter who it is: a harassing predator or a false accuser.

Now let's move on to #MeToo.

The founders of the #MeToo movement were right to speak up when they did. They gave other women the courage to come forward.

However, some of the self-proclaimed leaders of the movement have hurt their cause by advocating that all women's accusations should be believed all the time.

Just as not all men should be believed, neither should all women. We instinctively know this, as we all know game-playing manipulators in both genders. In the abstract, the #MeToo leadership comments sound good, even noble. But to impart the presumption of truth based on gender? Every person reading this can call out specific names of people who they absolutely know do not deserve being bestowed with credibility. And when lives and careers are in the balance, fairness and accuracy matters.

Every accuser should have their allegations and evidence reviewed with grave seriousness. But putting a thumb on the scale in investigations? It's a dangerous idea that goes against fairness, impartiality, and human instinct. People lie and arsonists exploit. And it provides a roadmap for arsonists.

If you give arsonists an upper hand and victories, expect problems to multiply. If you give them an inch, they'll take a mile. They pervert the system and use a process designed for use by good and decent people for their own indecent results.

Both women and men are badly hurt by false accusers, as women with complaints have their claims looked at with skepticism, and men who are falsely accused are tarnished as well.

The battle is helping no one, and it's getting worse.

A post-#MeToo survey by LeanIn and SurveyMonkey surveyed 3,000 employed adults about attitudes toward the opposite sex in the workplace. They found that nearly half of male managers are "uncomfortable mentoring, socializing, or working alone with women."[3]

This has been an open secret, but people are starting to talk about it more and more. Why is this happening?

For some men—particularly those who are concerned about false accusations—legal protections aren't enough. It's also about protecting reputations. One of those men is Vice President Mike Pence. The "Pence Rule," as it has been come to be known, is his practice of never meeting with a woman alone under any circumstance. Pence was mocked for this policy by the media, political leaders, and women's advocates for what they believed to be an ignorant view of working with women. And you may believe that as well. But as with other decisions in a business setting, reducing your exposure to risk is a big deal. It's why we pay insurance and why we plan strategically to avoid mistakes in the business world. Did I just reduce men and women in the workplace to risk assessment? Yes, and it's the type of assessment businesses make every day. And in life. Men are scared and the "believe all women" mantra scares the daylights out of them. If you are presumed guilty, you are going to operate from a defensive posture and reduce your risk of getting in trouble. It's today's reality.

I know from dozens of conversations with corporate contacts—all of them off the record—that many men in the business and political worlds operate under some offshoot of the Pence Rule already. Others who are more relaxed still make sure to always have someone else in the room wherever a meeting takes place. And others have their list in their mind of whom they are willing to be in an elevator alone with and whom they have some doubts about. This situation harms the numerous women who I have proudly worked with every day. And the atmosphere is caused not only by the harassers, but also the few, but impactful, false accusers.

Ultimately, I believe that in a highly charged era of social media, in which people have the ability to upload things to the internet in seconds, no one should expect people *not* to protect themselves from frivolous accusations in one way or another—and maybe that is an area where we can find common ground.

We have two realities today in the #MeToo era. First, women are being harmed because some companies with a large percentage of men in the senior ranks are now in defensive mode, and women are losing out on networking, leadership, and mentoring opportunities because men are in a defensive crouch. Some companies—mainly smaller operations—are moving to a "no women" staffing policy once you reach a certain level of the company. Second, men are concerned and have reason to be, with a believe-all-women mindset among some activist groups that get a sympathetic ear from the media.

Bloomberg reporters Gillian Tan and Katia Porzecanski broke a December 3, 2018, story entitled "Wall Street Rule for the #MeToo Era: Avoid Women at All Cost" and laid out the problem well that women now face.

The article begins, "No more dinners with female colleagues. Don't sit next to them on flights. Book hotel rooms on different floors. Avoid one-on-one meetings. Across Wall Street, men are adopting controversial strategies for the #MeToo era and, in the process, making life even harder for women."[4]

The problems with this situation are plentiful. Women are being hurt, men have legitimate concerns, and no one is talking about solutions. Instead, both sides, much like our political system, are appealing to their base supporters. And I haven't even talked about the companies that have unwritten policies to not hire women. As someone who has seen what the effects of having an accusatory arsonist within an organization can do as well as a father of a brilliant, talented daughter, I both am horrified and understanding of that policy. No one wants to be the person brought down by an arsonist, and to prevent it from happening means a lot of people are taking powerful, insulating measures to keep it from happening.

Let me play mediator.

If business leaders were sitting across from me, I'd tell them this:

> Gentlemen, we have a problem: It's not right that women you trust are being frozen out of meetings that they have earned a seat in because of a "one size fits all" policy that is easier than having tough discussions on personnel. Also, know that the sexual harassment suit you are trying to avoid may be replaced with a sex discrimination suit if you've instituted women-free corporate zones within your company as a tacit policy. If you're freezing women out summarily, end the practice. Tighten up your company's harassment policies to make them squeaky clean, and have no tolerance for predatory behavior. And let's all agree—both sexes—on what harassment is and isn't. Surely our society can come up with a definition everyone understands and can operate under. Be on the frontlines of empowering women and bringing your best and brightest women into the fold at all levels of your organizations.

My message to the women would be just as succinct:

> Please understand that men have legitimate concerns about protecting themselves from false accusations. Much as virtue, respect, and your career are of importance to you, they're also just as important to men. The media has had a "shoot first, ask questions later" approach regarding sensational charges in the work-

place. That is fine in valid cases, but it's poisonous in the case of false accusations. We need to marginalize and denounce rhetoric that says all men should be assumed guilty and fight for systems that are fair, thorough, and tough on both harassers and false accusers.

If we can get the loud fringe voices out of the game and onto the sidelines, workplaces will get better, and consensus will likely be found. The middle ground I have laid out will solve most of the biggest problems.

One last thing on sexual harassment and the battles of the sexes in the workplace: Let's stop pretending we can micromanage everything. When we do, whether as organizations or as individuals, we tend to look really clumsy and really dumb.

Reeling from a scandal that knocked Kevin Spacey from his leading role in *House of Cards*, Netflix created an internal policy to stop abusive and harassing behaviors. While those behaviors are, of course, objectionable, sending a group of consultants into a room and expecting them to solve thousands of years of male-female interaction is ridiculous. When they do this, they look like a bad meme. Netflix did just that with their ham-handed effort. Good intentions, bad look.

Netflix's rules for the workplace road, according to *The Sun,* include

- Do not look at anyone for more than five seconds.

- Shout "Stop, don't do that again" if someone is being inappropriate.

- Don't give lingering hugs or touch anyone for a lengthy period of time.

- Don't flirt.

- Don't ask for a colleague's phone number.

- Steer clear of a colleague once they have said they are not interested in you.

- *Report* a colleague who has given anyone unwanted attention.[5]

Netflix's rules, all undoubtedly well-intentioned, create a new layer of definitions for the workplace to monitor: look length, hug duration, phone number purposing regulation, instructions to shout when uncomfortable, and the establishment of a reporting process.

I understand their point, but pretty please, corporate community—don't do things like this. You can control a lot, but can we agree that the new role of management is not to be pulling out the stopwatch for five-second look rules? You make all the sensible attempts at dealing with difficult issues look silly.

In my case, if only the firm could have given me the responsibility to write a list. Maybe I'd have started with a "Don't follow your coworker" policy.

Oh, we haven't talked about that one yet? Stay tuned.

Chapter Five

ME AND MY SHADOW— AND THE ARSONIST'S APPRENTICE

They say sometimes that truth is stranger than fiction. I think each can give the other a run for its money.

Fast-forward a few months after the lunch. I had just experienced a very successful run of projects and was too busy to keep an eye on Hazel's antics on a daily basis. She had launched numerous disruptions here and there, but nothing out of the ordinary, at least for Hazel. Despite the drama, we had had a successful year in Congress. Now it was time to toot our own horn and talk about the firm's successes and those of our clients during the session. That's Lobbying 101. Good news or bad news, you have to explain things early and often to legislators about what your clients are doing. If you don't, your opponents will run you over. That's politics.

That meant I was scheduling lots of meetings with members

of Congress all over the country in their home districts. All it took was me sitting down in my office, making a call, and deciding whether we'd meet over lunch or breakfast.

In one particularly busy week, I had a meeting with Congressman Bo Cockerham, favorite son of the majestic city of Minnetonka, Minnesota. We met for lunch at Reilly's Roast Beef, his favorite hole-in-the-wall in his district. On the day of the lunch, I flew in, drove straight to Minnetonka, and over to Reilly's. I got a table early and waited for the congressman and his team. When Cockerham and his team arrived, we shook hands, positioned ourselves around the table, and ordered our lunch. The waiter disappeared to put our order in, and as we began to talk, a familiar voice cut through the lunchtime buzz like a chainsaw through a tree.

"Oh. My. God! What are you guys doing here?"

Icy fingers of dread trailed down my back. Hazel, clad in parka and boots, had shown up in Minnetonka.

Waving her arms wildly as if she were hoping to achieve flight, she quickly reduced our meeting to how it was *so amazing* and *such a coincidence* that we were having lunch in the *same restaurant* at the *same time* in the *same state* on the *same day.*

Cockerham appeared to be perplexed and amused. I promised him a meeting but had not mentioned that I was tossing in a sideshow.

"Quite a coincidence, Hazel," I said, concealing my real thoughts. "Who are you meeting here?"

"I have a lunch with, umm, Ted Underhill, you know, from Minnetonka Meat Packing."

"I didn't know we worked with Minnetonka Meat Packing," I said.

"What are the odds?" I asked, knowing exactly what the

odds were—microscopic.

She shook her head vigorously with a dizzying yes. "I know! I just reached out to him! Can you believe it?"

While the conversation was hijacked and diverted to Hazel, I did the mental math on the chances of Hazel and me being in the same place at the same time on the same day. I should have bought every lottery ticket in Minnesota.

After a quick glance, my way revealed I welcomed her presence as much as people welcome a kidney stone, she sprayed the table with a round of business cards before beating a hasty retreat. "It was so much fun to see all of you!" she said.

How supremely odd. No one there other than someone with an understanding of Hazel's track record would have ever considered that she was intentionally showing up for any reason other than coincidence because, well, no one purposefully appears at other people's meetings. Right? It's odd. It's unusual. It's highly inappropriate and so outside of the norm that few would ever consider that someone was doing that. I never had, up until this point in my life. Yet here she was, and I needed to rule out random chance as the cause.

Her actions reminded me of Frank Abagnale, whose life story was captured in the film *Catch Me If You Can*. A master deceiver and con artist, Abagnale inserted himself into numerous situations by having the shamelessness to act in ways other people never would. Abagnale posed as a doctor, lawyer, and copilot despite not even being eighteen years old! Despite his actions being criminal, he thought of his actions as simply playing a role. While not engaging in the criminal, Hazel had a similar shamelessness. It's amazing what someone can do if they have no fear of getting caught—or in Hazel's case, no fear of punishment if she did get caught. They feel liberated. Not necessarily to break the law, but most assuredly to break every norm of business and acceptable interaction.

I had no doubt that Hazel had arranged to be at the same location for lunch, but the question remained: How did she know the details? She was either accessing my calendar or eavesdropping on my calls. We shared a wall in common, and unless we were whispering, we could usually hear what was being said in the other person's office. I had tuned her conversations out, but it appeared she found my comments much more interesting. I'd placed the call to Congressman Cockerham for this meeting while I was sitting in my office.

There was one way to find out. It was time to set a trap.

A few days after the Minnetonka Mambo when I was back at the firm, I waited until Hazel was in her office and made an imaginary phone call. I picked up the phone and wheeled my chair close to the wall. I began to speak loudly, at least louder than usual, to the imaginary version of the "Pride of Pawtucket, Rhode Island," Congressman Russell Kolip.

"Hey, Representative Kolip," I said. "Fantastic to talk to you again. It's good to be out of the Washington swamp and back in Pawtucket, right? Did you have a chance to look over the material I sent you about establishing the federal death penalty for those who drive unnecessarily in the left lane? Uh huh. Mmm, hmm. Yes, sir, I agree. Since I would like you to be a key sponsor, I would like to meet with you in the next week or two in the district. A lunch? Why sure, next Wednesday would be great! Royal Pandemonium Pizzeria at eleven-thirty right down the street from your office? That's one of my favorites! I saw it profiled on that TV show *Pasta, Pesto, and Pizzerias!* See you then."

I loudly placed the receiver down on the cradle. With that, the trap was set.

As the week wore on, the wait was killing me. This wasn't

exactly a solving a "crime of the century" type of moment, but I just had to see how this would play out.

I flew into Providence the night before the faux meeting and stayed at one of Pawtucket's finest hotels. I had some other appointments scheduled, so the "lunch" was a perfect fit into my busy day. Late that morning, I drove over to the restaurant, picked a table in the back of the main dining area, and ordered an appetizer. I had a feeling I wouldn't be waiting long.

I was right.

Like clockwork, just few minutes after the imaginary Congressman Kolip and friends were supposed to arrive, a particularly pugnacious paragon of impropriety held court at the hostess table.

After obviously not getting the information she wanted from the hostess, she began to enter each of the private meeting rooms—the type of section in a restaurant where I usually held my briefings—though not on this particular day. For this meeting, I wanted to be right in the middle of all the action. As Hazel began looking around the restaurant, I stared at my food. Where was she going next?

A minute later, I looked up again and saw that Hazel had parked herself in an adjacent room. All I could see from my view was her high-heeled shoes that peeked out from along the wall separating the two rooms. Hazel couldn't see me, but she had a great view of the front door. She was ready to spring into action whenever Kolip made his appearance.

I then spent the next hour letting Hazel luxuriate in the uncertainty. The feet told the story. Fidgeting. Tapping. Feet crossing and uncrossing. Her movements were as varied as her moods. While I was enjoying the moment, it was time for me to wrap this up and get the rest of my day started. I walked over to Hazel's room at the restaurant, supremely happy to engage.

"Hazel!" I said, feigning surprise. "Is that you? What are you doing here? What are the odds? How exciting to see you! What a coincidence. Again. For the second time in a few weeks. In a random state at the same restaurant."

Hazel was caught flat-footed. The usual machine-gun wordsmithing that I normally witnessed from her slowed to a halting cadence. Shifting in her seat, playing with her hair, and feet moving in all directions, Hazel was doing everything but making eye contact. She was swallowing her soft drink like she was in a competition.

"Oh! Hi, Pete, what are you doing here? I'm ha—"

I cut her off. "Were you expecting Congressman Kolip? If so, I haven't talked with him in a couple of months. But I'm so excited you came to join me in Pawtucket."

Her face went deadly serious. "I don't appreciate all the questions. I'm waiting on my guest to arrive for my meeting, and this is embarrassing," she said.

With a heartfelt "Have some pizza, Hazel. You'll love it!" I bid her farewell, left a tip for the waiter, and headed out to finish the rest of my day's work.

While most smelled garlic and the wafting aromatic greatness that was the pizzeria's marinara, I smelled victory. It was the last time Hazel showed up at one of my meetings.

I had embarrassed her into retreat by speaking her language of deceit. It seemed to be what she understood. Having a deep colleague-to-colleague chat about the principled merits of not showing up at your colleague's meetings like a character in *Single While Female* wouldn't have stopped her. Exposing her as a fraud by dragging her to the other side of the country to realize she had just been called out? Now that did the trick.

Once back in the office, I stopped by Suzy's office for a chat about my colleague's scheduling "coordination."

"Suzy, I don't even know where to begin with what I'm about to say. But . . . Hazel is showing up at my lunch meetings uninvited and unannounced."

"Is that a problem?" she asked.

That set me back on my heels.

I better try that again. Surely she misunderstood.

"I may not have been clear enough," I said. "I am setting up private meetings with elected officials, and Hazel is showing up—out of nowhere. She was not invited. You don't find that odd?"

I continued. "She came to the first meeting with Congressman Cockerham a few weeks ago unannounced in Minnesota and said it was a coincidence. It's on the other side of the planet! Last week, I announced on a phone call just loud enough for her to hear that I had a lunch with Congressman Kolip in Pawtucket, Rhode Island, and she showed up again."

"She may just feel like you're avoiding her," Suzy offered. "Get her involved. No matter what she's done in the past, she loves being part of a team."

In a nonsensical conversation like this, the normal instinct would be to wait for a few seconds as the host of the reality show walks in to let you know they were playing a gag on you. But not here. "Suzy, if I overheard you saying you had a lunch meeting with someone and I showed up unannounced, would you find that unusual? No, you would get a restraining order!" I said.

"I feel for what you're saying, but we always need to think of Hazel," she said.

"Will you explain to her that this is unacceptable?" I asked.

"I just want us all to be a team," said Suzy. I swear I could almost hear "Kumbaya" somewhere in the distance.

It was then I realized I had more than one problem in the

firm. While I had been busy working on legislative successes in Washington and elsewhere for months, Suzy had suddenly become a living, breathing motivational-speaker talking point. Suzy's concerns about managing Hazel were a distant second to surviving her. Suzy did not want to become that next buried body, so her solution to managing Hazel became pretending that anything she did was perfectly normal—a cognitive dissonance that knew no bounds. I had both sympathy for her plight and was stunned by her lack of leadership all at the same time.

Arsonists are a cancer in a toxic workplace, but so are their enablers. And the enablers usually wield some level of power. They hold the matches and the gas can while the fire is being lit. Wittingly or unwittingly, they accelerate and spread an arsonist's fires. That was Suzy. A firm survivalist and within sight of her retirement nirvana, she had become the arsonist's apprentice.

Chapter Six

FIREPROOFING YOUR HIRING PROCESS

I was exhausted from the drama, and I haven't even told you half of it yet. I was the target of some of Hazel's actions, but I wasn't subsidizing it, either. What is management thinking when it let an arsonist run wild? They are literally paying the costs of arsonists.

Those entanglements must really be costly or embarrassing, I often thought.

Wouldn't things be much easier if you never had to work with or manage the arsonist in the first place?

Dealing with a Hazel can be all consuming, so the best way to avoid the problem is to fireproof your hiring process—and keep the arsonists out!

In their October 2015 paper "Toxic Workers," Professor Dylan Minor and Cornerstone on Demand's Michael Housman noted that about 5 percent of all workers end up getting terminated for serious offenses—bullying, falsifying documents, embezzling funds, severe harassment, and similar toxic behaviors.[1]

Information like this begs the question: How do we keep that 5 percent out of organizations in the first place?

Most people who study this question agree that observing personality traits and competent research at the beginning of the hiring process are the best ways to screen out toxic employees. Minor and his co-author tracked the data of close to 60,000 workers and found a few early warning signs:

- An obsession with rules. Following procedures is one thing. Not showing any understanding or appreciation for gray areas is another. These people may be trying to cover up their own propensity to break those rules. Remember the phrase in *Hamlet*, "The lady (or gentleman) doth protest too much, methinks."

- Peacock-like displays of excessive overconfidence. You may be dealing with someone who believes rules don't apply to him or her. The overconfidence could also mean they believe they will never be caught.

- The world revolves around them, and they're happy to let you know it. Listen for how many sentences the person begins with the word *I* or end with the word *me*. Or credit in stories that only goes to one person—them.[2]

To find out what and whom you're dealing with, it's important to ask questions that clue you in to an applicant's mindset. "Tell me about your biggest mistake," for example, will yield insight into the ability of a person to be self-analytical or whether they'll be throwing people under the bus for their mistakes if hired. "What was your least favorite thing about your previous employer?" will tell you if they understand discretion. Remember that history repeats itself. Whatever this person is saying now about his or her prior company could be said about your company in a few years.[3]

The *personality* of the applicant is important. Are they positive, team-oriented, and enthusiastic? Some of the best organizational cultures we know of are ones that hire for personality and work from there.

One well-documented way to avoid hiring mistakes is to let great employees in the company have a role in hiring. They know what kind of people they get along with and who they think will be a problem. This type of thinking is at the heart of employee referral programs. Companies with strong referral programs tend to have higher retention rates and stronger employee engagement than companies that don't. It's not rocket science. Good people tend to want to be around other good people.

Just as important as getting your best employees to encourage their friends to join the company is keeping toxic employees from having a major decision-making role in the hiring process. Why? Toxic behavior spreads fast, and toxic people want people like themselves. If you're a *Star Trek* fan, you probably remember "The Trouble with Tribbles."

In that episode, Captain Kirk and the crew of the *Enterprise* are enjoying a day of relaxation on a faraway planet. While there, Lt. Uhura finds a tribble—a small furry pet that appears harmless. But once on board, however, the tribbles begin to multiply exponentially, eat all food on the ship, and attack the systems that allowed the *Enterprise* to function. Tribbles are indeed trouble, and they multiply! Toxic employees, if you let them, can multiply as well. Don't bring aboard toxic tribbles!

Of course, keeping toxic employees in place has problems

far beyond one troublemaker's actions. They infect others. A March 2018 *Harvard Business Review* study by Stephen Dimmock and William Gerken found that retaining toxic employees or adding them to your ranks can multiply an organization's problems.[4] Toxicity, though often compared to a cancer, is also like the flu in some ways. It's contagious!

Dimmock and Gerken collected and studied regulatory filings for financial advisors who had paid financial settlements or lost in arbitration because of unethical professional practices. They then watched what happened next. They found that advisors were 37 percent more likely to commit some kind of misconduct if they started working with someone with a history of previous misconduct.[5] In other words, mixing toxic employees with non-toxic employees usually creates more toxic employees.

Charles Schwab CEO Walt Bettinger offers a great way to smoke out toxic behaviors and find employees he wants. In an interview with Adam Bryant of the *New York Times*, Bettinger revealed that he sometimes meets prospective employees for breakfast as a way to learn more about them and watch them in a real-life setting.

> One thing I'll do sometimes is meet someone for breakfast for the interview. I'll get there early, pull the manager of the restaurant aside, and say, "I want you to mess up the order of the person who's going to be joining me. It'll be OK, and I'll give a good tip, but mess up their order. "I do it because I want to see how the person responds. That will help me understand how they deal with adversity. Are they upset, are they frustrated, or are they understanding? Life is like that, and business is like that. It's just another way to get a look inside their heart rather than their head. We're all going to make mistakes.

The question is, how are we going to recover when we make them, and are we going to be respectful to others when they make them?[6]

Without taking analysis of Bettinger's erroneous omelet interviews to an extreme, the process makes complete sense. He gets to see how someone treats challenges and people before they're hired. If you want to see how someone deals with challenges, put them in a setting where you can see them in action.

Additionally, take the reference check review process seriously. It's incredible how many companies rely on an applicant's three hand-picked references as a major basis for their hiring. Does anyone really think that employees are providing any names that will have anything negative to say? Be better than that in the hiring process. Ask applicants for more specific references that will help you find out who these candidates really are.

Finally, if you have a toxic employee slip through the cracks in the hiring process and you identify the problem, act swiftly, and remove them early on. If you don't address obvious problems, you are literally institutionalizing indecision and leaving the Suzys of the C-suite to deal with serious problems.

Chapter Seven

HOT OFF THE PRESSES

With this chapter alone, I may help thousands of companies retain their employees who are on the fence about looking for another job. Who would want to take the chance on what will happen in your next job if they have a chance of running into what I'm about to describe?

I may be going out on a limb here, but I believe one truth of life is that you know you are in an unusual professional environment when your daily life starts to sound like a *Scooby Doo* cartoon.

As I headed back in after a long weekend, I walked into the office, saying hi to colleagues and getting ready for a week of non-stop activity. Nothing was extraordinary. People were chatting, typing, talking, slurping coffee, and blending in among a sea of cubicles.

Once in my office, I put my computer bag on the floor and noticed a book in my chair. I assumed it was client-related material, but then I looked a little closer.

A taped-on piece of paper covered the title. Printed or typed onto the paper, it said: "Pete, read this if you're going to survive Hazel."

No name on it.

"What the heck is this?" I said out loud to nobody in particular.

I sat there staring at the note. I was fascinated. Someone had typed a note and then taped it to the cover. Why type something when they could just write eight simple words? Surely it wasn't a fear of someone having their handwriting identified, was it? As silly as it sounds and as much as I wanted to discount it, the Secret Squirrel, uber-paranoid level at the firm made that thought entirely plausible.

I pulled off the note and read the title: *The Sociopath Next Door,* by Martha Stout. I had little knowledge about what a sociopath was at that point, though I had heard the term used numerous times over the years and soldiered through a class in Psych 101.

As a quick aside, let me be clear: In this chapter, I am not diagnosing anyone or anything. I am not a psychotherapist, psychiatrist, or counselor. I am only relating the facts of my experience and a truly bizarre professional experience.

Imagine it. In any normal office, your coworkers might haze you about how badly your favorite football team played over the weekend. Or they might decorate your office on your birthday. You might get a magazine article left on your desk or stuck on your bulletin board when somebody reads something interesting.

But me? I got books about the danger of sociopaths.

Are you feeling better about your current job yet?

It was going to be a busy day, so I put the book in my bag to be my homework for the night. I put it out of my mind multiple times that day, but I couldn't help but have it creep back in. I kept thinking someone would "out" themselves. I walked around reading faces, gauging reactions, trying to spot anything that might betray the stealthy Samaritan's action.

I even asked a few colleagues that I was personally close to if they were playing a prank on me by giving me the book or if they had seen anything.

No such luck.

I went home without any answers. Before I dug into the book, I looked at the reviews on Amazon. Crime novelist Jonathan Kellerman said: "*The Sociopath Next Door* is a chillingly accurate portrayal of evil—the decent person's guide to indecency."[1]

How bad are things at work when someone thinks a book with a review from a crime novelist should be required reading for you?

I picked up the book and looked it over—the cover, the back page—and gave it a quick flip-through to get a feel for the length. It felt like a night-long read.

While the book looked new, someone had highlighted, circled, and underlined various sections. Someone had left breadcrumbs for me to follow.

Over the next few weeks, I read every word multiple times. I learned that the most basic characteristic of a sociopath is the willingness or even desire to disregard the rights and feelings of others. Sociopaths dominate to get what they want—sex, money, possessions, businesses, promotions or approval. They love the feeling of being in control. They lack a conscience. They impress with big promises, big plans, and big stories. I learned that sociopaths often are not the people that they initially present themselves to be. I learned that sociopaths enjoy scapegoating and get their kicks from causing pain and watching people in pain. They alternate between extreme charm and extreme intimidation. And that they can be extremely successful professionally because they are not inhibited by the ethical, moral, or behavioral constraints that stop people from stepping on others on their way to success.[2]

Most of all, I learned how to spot destructive personality traits. To do that means you have to ignore a person's words and instead watch their behavior.[3] It's a little like playing defense in football—if you want to know a quarterback's true intentions on what they plan to do, watch their eyes. With people, the best way to get a read on them is to watch their actions, not their words. With Hazel, nice words and happy sayings were usually a smokescreen for what was actually happening.

The behaviors I witnessed made me search for answers. And I wasn't wondering only about Hazel's behavior. Suzy's actions became essential to watch as well.

One day, in the middle of a meeting with Suzy; the head of filing, Freda; the head of payroll, Patty; and me, Hazel's name came up incidentally.

"Why are we talking about Hazel? Is something wrong?" Suzy said.

"I have nothing to say about that woman, baby. I plead the fifth," said Freda the finance whiz. She was a woman about Hazel's age, and her tone left no doubt about where she stood.

"I'm not poking that bear," said the head of payroll, Patty.

I kept quiet. I only talked about Hazel if I absolutely had to.

After several seconds of awkward silence, Freda chimed in with a chuckle. "Pete, you're pretty quiet. Tell us what you think about your friend next door."

I played it safe with a neutral "She's very good at what she does."

"You don't have to say anything else, Pete. We're all friends here," said Patty.

To my surprise, Suzy jumped back into the conversation with force. "I don't want to hear any more discussion about Hazel," she said, locking eyes with me to let me know that this order included me.

"Nobody is attacking Hazel," Freda said.

Suzy snapped back. "I don't care. We shouldn't be talking about people when they're not here to defend themselves."

"Fair enough," I said.

"Fine," said Patty.

It was a strange moment. Suzy's defensiveness was understandable because she had nothing to gain from managing Hazel but plenty to lose. Managing Hazel meant Suzy would eventually be attacked by her. Not reining Hazel in brought an understandable lack of respect from some colleagues, but it helped her stay on track for her Emeritus Partner retirement package. What a humiliating pair of options to pick from. She chose to become Hazel's defender.

On days like this, I felt like I was watching Stockholm syndrome in action.

Stockholm syndrome is a psychological phenomenon exhibited in the wake of a bank robbery in Stockholm, Sweden in the early 1970s. People who had been taken hostage during a bank robbery refused to testify against their captors. The hostages even publicly defended the criminals, speaking of their humanity and goodness. At the firm, Hazel was the captor, Suzy the hostage, and Cecil had long since fled the crime scene.

If Stockholm syndrome does not click with you, let's call it "Schultz syndrome." Fans of the 1960s TV show *Hogan's Heroes* might better understand "Schultz syndrome," a condition I hereby name after the sweet but pathetic German guard best known for his "I see nothing! I hear nothing! I know nothing!"[4] denials of what he saw the show's prisoners of war doing. The prisoners could be in the middle of an escape, and Schultz would see them. But he didn't want to admit he was seeing a darn thing. He just wanted to get through the war in peace!

Shortly after the Freda/Patty meeting, Suzy told me that she wanted to schedule a new meeting to discuss that meeting. Meetings to discuss meetings—efficiency at its finest.

The time came, and I knocked on Suzy's door. She waved me in. Suzy was at her desk surrounded by numerous boxes, stacks of paper, and her now-familiar tower of three-ring binders. As we revved up the small-talk portion of the meeting, her shuffling of the items on her desk began to look like the actions of a blackjack dealer on their tenth cup of coffee.

I shut the door and sat down in my usual spot.

"So, how's things?" Shuffle. Shuffle. Staple. Stack.

"Busy," I said truthfully.

"You like your job?" Reach. Stack. Toss. Search. Stack. Shuffle. Crumble. Stack. Stack.

I nodded. "Every day is an adventure. You weren't wrong!"

We chatted about other parts of the job and, in a major change, even discussed people at the firm not named Hazel. That didn't last long.

"I'd also like to discuss Hazel," she said. "If you're game."

Womp. Womp. Womp.

"Pete," she said, "you were hired to make peace with Hazel, and you haven't made peace."

"Yeah, I know. Combat pay."

"We've talked about what she does to people, right?" said Suzy.

"Yes, you have told me many times. I am professional

with Hazel, but I avoid unnecessarily talking to her other than when I need to do my job. She shows up at my meetings! And we haven't discussed anything about the lunch we had! I think you may be making things more dysfunctional by giving her actions legitimacy and rationalizing some very strange behaviors," I said.

"More dysfunctional? You're saying this department is dysfunctional?" said Suzy.

Don't answer that! Don't answer that! Don't answer that! I thought. *Don't hit that softball!*

"Suzy, just wait here," I said.

And so began the first meeting of the firm's book club.

I walked down the hall, grabbed my copy of *The Sociopath Next Door*, and strode back to her office. I handed her my now well-used copy. She looked at the cover and paused pensively. I thought I would hear the same dodge, defend, and distract type of banter I had grown to expect. Instead, by the end of the meeting, I halfway expected her to ask me to lie down and tell her about my childhood.

Suzy set the book down and leaned back in her chair. She was more relaxed than I had ever seen her. I had no idea where the conversation was about to take us, but I thought I'd lead off.

"Suzy, someone thinks this should be my operations manual for working here. They put this in my office and said I need to read it to survive. What does that say to you?" I said.

"Pete, let's talk about this. Did you read it?" said Suzy. "What did you think?"

"I read it," I said. "I haven't read anything quite like it."

"That's fair, but you must have some opinions," she added, proceeding to go on for a while on some subjects I knew little to nothing about.

Suzy began to relate a long analysis of all things Hazel. It was a *tour de force* that made me more than a little uncomfortable. I certainly wasn't a fan of Hazel, but I also felt that Suzy was on highly uncomfortable terrain in discussing an employee. A malignant what? A congenital who? She referenced the subject matter as easily as I rattle off lines from movies. Statistics and suppositions were no match that day for her roam through the dramatic, disturbing, and diagnostic. She powerwalked through a litany of characteristics and behaviors, the same ones I'd just learned from the book and vaguely remembered from random articles I had seen posted on social media over the years.

Then she finally ended the spiel. "So, Pete, what I'm trying to say is that I don't really know what Hazel is."

I sat there, speechless.

The faint sound of crickets filled the room.

Suzy continued. "Some of this is really fluid, and there are a lot of debates on exactly how many characteristics somebody needs to have before they are grouped into one category or another, or not in a category at all."

I listened as Suzy broke down terms that were of interest to her: Grandiosity, idealism, narcissism, megalomania, codependency, and superiority complexes. Some she tossed out as perhaps relevant, others were just part of the show, I guess. She hypothesized about Hazel's possession or lack of possession of behavioral traits like she was mixing and matching outfits on a Barbie doll.

I sat there, desperately trying to think of an excuse to get out of the room. Suzy was quite the amateur analyst. All she needed was a pipe, a tweed jacket, and an armchair.

Finally, she turned the conversation back to me. "I've gone on for far too long. You should've stopped me, Pete.

"Tell me, what are you thinking?"

Pass!

"I really don't know what to think," I replied, "but I never thought I would be playing 'Name That Diagnosis' with my boss."

She nodded agreement. "Yes, life isn't always what we expect. You kind of roll with the punches."

"It sounds like you really know a lot about psychology, Suzy."

"I like finding out what makes people tick. Personality tests, things like that. You can learn so much."

"I should be reading psychology books?" I asked.

"Oh, yes. Educate yourself. It's the differences we all have that make life fun."

Yeah, I'm having a great time, I thought. I just had to ask the question that was killing me to keep inside. I took a deep breath and went for broke.

"Suzy, did you give me this book?"

Suzy looked stunned—and I was pretty stunned too. I had just asked a question that put her in a very uncomfortable position, but the question needed to be asked.

I sat silent, awaiting her response and noticed her paper shuffling operation had ground to a halt. She looked around as though she had lost her keys somewhere on her desk, but it was her thought process and ability to speak that had turned up missing. Seas parted. I may have grown a beard during this lull. The Browns may have won a Super Bowl or two. It was the lull that would not end.

"Suzy?"

The response drought continued. After an excruciatingly long several minutes, just before I was about to call in a team of medics to check her vitals, Suzy shook her head "no" for a brief nanosecond.

Then, finally, she spoke. And nothing about my question.

"So how's your daughter enjoying school?" she said, apropos of precisely nothing.

The force of the swing and a miss on my question knocked me over

"She's doing very well. Math is her favorite, and she loves writing, too." I responded, amused and stunned.

"Of course, of course. I love math. I was pretty good at it. Not enough to become a mathematician or anything," said Suzy.

"Suzy, I asked about the book."

"Let's talk again soon," she said.

"OK, Suzy," I said, hoping a meteor would strike and put an end to this meeting

Suzy walked around her desk, sat down, and began working as though I wasn't even in the room.

I exited the office, a little shaken and slightly amused, but going forward I really had reason to wonder about who was giving me psychology books.

Chapter Eight

HOW ALARMING IS YOUR TOXIC COWORKER? FROM MILDLY BAD TO DARK TRIAD

Not everyone is going to work with a Hazel, but the odds are really good that you will have a destructive person—even an arsonist—in your life someday.

Toxicity can come in lots of shapes and sizes and, if you're reading this book, you know from your own experience that there are many types of toxic workers around the organizations, including:

1. The Belittlers—These people hurl insults and putdowns at every opportunity. They're better than you and their work is, too—just ask them!

2. The Credit Thieves—They take all the public glory for other people's hard work. It's by design to put others in

a lower position compared to them and to help them move up the food chain. In an interview, if you're being inundated with "I, I, I," make a note.

3. The Finger Pointers—They deflect blame onto others when things go wrong. They also tend to be among the biggest saboteurs in an organization. Remember, a question on professional challenges they faced previously or questions about their past managers may smoke them out in an interview.

4. The Gossips—These people spread gossip, lies, half-truths, and whatever else they can find to create chaos through their constant chatter. While some cannot stop talking out of habit, others gossip with an agenda. Because of the agenda-driven gossips, always be careful about what you say to anyone at work. If you do not want your personal life, or what you thought were private comments about people at work, to spread to everyone else in the company, don't say anything worth spreading! Also, don't be seen around gossips if you don't want to be labeled as one. If you get branded as a gossip, expect to catch some of the blame when one of the gossips goes too far. You'll be an immediate suspect and lose people's trust. Tough to detect in the interview process, managers should be prepared to step in when the Gossips become a problem.

5. The Wet Blankets—These buzzkills may not be productive, but they excel at complaining and criticizing. They steal people's joy, complain about pay raises not being big enough, and pick apart successful initiatives. They also may look to rain on your parade when it comes to acknowledging your accomplishments. Since one of the

most important things teams can do to form bonds is celebrate victories, these folks can hurt your company's morale—in good times and bad. You can try to filter them out in the interview process through questions that help you understand whether they are going to be a positive force within the organization—or not.

6. The Slackers—They shrug off responsibilities and leave them to others. It starts early in life—probably with group projects at school where one student slacks off and the rest of the group is left to pick up the slack. Don't worry, though. They'll help you out in accepting the credit!

7. The Leeches—They want your time and your labor. They're using you and are taking credit for the work you provide them. They also create an unbalanced relationship that kills your productivity and throw drama your way if you stop answering their calls for help.

8. The High and Mighty—The High and Mighty are closed-minded and general know-it-alls. They are static personalities, as they believe that their perfection has already been reached and simply needs to be maintained. Think of John McEnroe, the spoiled brat of professional tennis in the 1970s and 1980s. Dr. Carol S. Dweck, professor of psychology at Stanford, summed him up in her book *Mindset*: "McEnroe did not love to learn. He did not thrive on challenges; when the going got rough, he often folded. As a result, by his own admission, he did not reach his own potential."[1] McEnroe achieved the number-one ranking in the world, but became best known for on-court temper tantrums which were often a cover for his own mistakes. McEnroe is a classic High and Mighty.

Spot them by asking in interviews about how well they fit at previous companies. If they're being truthful, they will usually already have a history of poor social skills and maladjustment to professional environments as well as poor references despite potentially great individual performance.

9. The Lone Wolf—This character doesn't fit in the office and doesn't want to try. He or she is out of step with everyone else, out of sight of everyone else, and sometimes out of his or her mind. Their spinal columns are seemingly made of steel because they cannot compromise or give in, being tremendous egotists. The challenge with dealing with the Lone Wolf is that this person is often a high performer.

10. The Drama Queen—Or, just as likely, the Drama King! Perpetually stuck in high school, this person thrives on information, news, or gossip. And, if there isn't enough news to go around, they'll make it up or twist the facts. Molehills are effortlessly turned into mountains. Unless you want your comments turned into the talk of the office, never tell them a word about your business. If you do, expect it to be used against you.

The top ten toxic tormentors in the workplace listed above are problematic at times, but they can be managed in most circumstances. Can you survive working with them under the right conditions? Sure, because if we ran from every person who annoyed us at one time or another, we'd live a very lonely existence.

But have you dealt with those whose actions are more disturbing and darker than nearly everyone else you have ever known? They're unforgettable, but not in a good way. Their actions chill a room. Cast a pall. Leave an indelible mark.

Their behavioral mega-quirks cannot be explained by substance abuse, troubles at home, or family background. They are manipulators, callous, void of empathy, and self-centered.

These disturbing behaviors may fall within what experts call the "Dark Triad." A trio of researchers from the University of British Columbia—Delroy Paulhus, Kevin Williams, and Peter Harms—described the triad in a landmark 2002 study.

The Dark Triad is composed of three disturbing overlapping behavioral traits: narcissism, Machiavellianism, and psychopathy.[2]

Narcissism, according to *Encyclopedia Britannica*, "is characterized by an inflated self-image and addiction to fantasy, by an unusual coolness and composure shaken only when narcissistic confidence is threatened and by the tendency to take others for granted or exploit them."[3] Numerous sources show they're drawn to leadership roles in business and other positions that can provide them visibility and financial rewards. Narcissists get their power by drawing people in through their strong personalities.

Machiavellianism was named for Niccolò Machiavelli, the author of *The Prince*. Dale Hartley, PhD, describes Machiavellianism as "a personality type that does not choose to be, but simply is, a master manipulator . . . They are temperamentally predisposed to be calculating, conniving and deceptive. Essentially amoral, they use other people as stepping stones to reach their goals."[4] They are not only good at manipulating, but they're drawn to jobs that allow them to manipulate others, including management, law, sales, and politics.

Psychopathy was defined by Henry R. Hermann, PhD, in his 2017 study "Dominance and Aggression in Humans and Other Animals" as "a mental disorder in which an individual manifests amoral and antisocial behavior, shows a lack of ability to love or establish meaningful relationships, expresses extreme egocentricity, and a failure to learn from experience. Considered the worst of the trio, and it is marked by *low empathy and high levels of impulsive thrill-seeking* [emphasis mine]."[5] A lack of remorse is a constant, and threats are often their superpower. Psychopaths have a tendency to eventually bottom out in their careers but can do well in positions where force of personality and cold and calculating decisions matter.

Change jobs a few times in your career and you will likely work with someone with Dark Triad traits. According to a recent edition of the *Diagnostic and Statistical Manual of Mental Disorders*, sociopathy is part of a group of "antisocial personality disorders" that make up approximately 3 percent of the population.[6] Other studies peg the percentage a little higher. In some types of work, their behaviors can even be a strength. It explains why Dark Triad types often perform very well in fields such as elite military units. What might work well in leading an anti-terrorist unit may not work in an accounting firm. This also explains why the Dark Triad types usually aren't found in fields that require a caring or empathetic interpersonal style, such as teaching or nursing.

In general, those with Dark Triad behaviors play out what's called a "fast-life strategy" that includes more sex partners, higher risk levels, short-term views, and limits on their self-control.

Another disorder is sociopathy. Sociopathy is similar to psychopathy according to most experts.

Sociopathic traits include the following characteristics:

• Excessive charm

• High IQ

- Lack of empathy

- No real emotions

- Egocentricities

- Calculating and cold

- Feelings of superiority

- Manipulative

- Compulsive lying

- Lover of loopholes

- Impulsive

- Adrenaline junkie

- Paranoid

- Hypersensitive to criticism

- An impersonal, trivial sex life[7]

Not every sociopath exhibits every one of the above traits. However, if you are seeing several of these traits, you have more than enough reason to be concerned.

Proceed with caution when working with Dark Triad types and would-be sociopaths. Learn how others in your department have dealt with the person you are concerned about. Many managers—heck, many mental health professionals—have no idea how to personally deal with the worst of the worst behavior patterns, so do not expect any game-changing answers. The managers may be just as scared and disturbed by an employee as you are. If that is the case, chart your path to move on to another department or job, or, if you choose to, use the tools in this book to be prepared for what may be a heck of a fight. Long-term exposure to those exhibiting Dark Triad traits can simply be bad for you in incalculable ways.

My thoughts? Good luck, watch out, and consider moving on. If your organization will not take action against the Dark Triad types when they cause problems and has left you to deal with them, plan your exit.

Chapter Nine

UNFRIENDLY FIRE

I sometimes felt like I had walked into the middle of a play, only everyone else had a script but me. This was one of those times.

After a congressional term in which our team had won some big victories, one of our clients, a ball bearings manufacturer, asked us to help put together a report to lawmakers about how they would implement a new law affecting their industry. That type of reporting is a common practice in my field, involving creation of a document and verbal testimony to one obscure congressional committee or another.

A few weeks before the report was due, Suzy sent me an email, saying Hazel had to be involved in helping put the report together. I wasn't surprised about the mandate from Suzy, but with Hazel's help came lots of headaches and surprises. The only question was when, not if, they happened.

It didn't take long to find out.

Suzy decided our trio would get together in her office to

determine what needed to be done and who would do which task. It was determined that I would take the lead.

When we sat down, the first sign of trouble was that there was no trouble. For two hours, we brainstormed, strategized, and put together a plan of attack. It was an entirely collegial manner—an oasis of normalcy and tranquility.

Nothing going wrong with Hazel meant something was very wrong. What would have appeared to be a paranoid thought before I joined the firm was now a viewpoint with a Nostradamus-like accuracy level.

After the meeting, I went back to my office and compiled the list of responsibilities we had agreed upon.

Once finished, I checked my email and saw a message from Suzy in my inbox.

Don't forget to share the responsibilities with Hazel!

And share I did. One for me. One for Hazel. One for me. One for Hazel.

I printed out the two lists and walked over to Hazel's office to give her five of our ten.

"Hazel, here's your list," I said. "It's evenly split. Let me know if you need anything else." Her assignments were just as mundane and boring as mine.

"OK," she said. Her eyes looked especially friendly that day.

What's going on? I thought.

"Any questions?" I asked.

"No, thanks," she said, once again grinning big.

Hmm . . . who are you, and what have you done with the real Hazel?

She was smiling as though she had just won the lottery.

"There's one thing on that list that I don't know how to do—the one with the PDF files. Do you know how to do that one?" I asked.

"Of course!" she said.

"Oh, good. Maybe you can teach me sometime."

She smiled sweetly again.

I left in a mild state of unease. This wasn't Hazel's default setting.

Within hours, there was a knock on my door. It was Suzy.

"Pete, please come down to my office," she said.

"When?"

"Right now."

I followed her down to her office. She waved me in and closed the door behind us.

"What's going on?" I asked.

Suzy sat behind her desk and composed herself. "There has been a complaint."

I didn't know the what, but I had a pretty good idea about the "who" part. "A complaint? Who has complained? About what?" I said.

"You've upset Hazel by assigning her a list of sexist tasks." Suzy waved the list in the air, now thick with grievance.

"Yes, I gave her half the tasks to complete, exactly what you told me to do," I said, biting my lip. "Where's the problem with that?

"It may be sexist exploitation."

I could feel my blood beginning to simmer, not yet at boiling. "Sexist exploitation? What does that mean?" My mental thesaurus was flipping through its pages and coming up dry.

"Historically speaking, administrative work has been assigned to women. Hazel believes it is sexist to ask her to do things you don't want to do. It's patriarchal behavior" she said.

I was annoyed but more exasperated. "Patriarchal!? I assigned *both* of us administrative work. It's *all* administrative work! That's what this project is. It's all administrative work. If

I'm being sexist to her, I'm being sexist to me, too.

"The list had ten things on it," I continued. "I got five. She got five. And what is this sexist exploitation thing again?"

"The PDF files. You made her do administrative work because she's a woman, she says."

"So Hazel's definition of *sexist* is what we are going with? I only assigned it to her because she said she knew how to do the PDF thing, and I don't!"

Suzy didn't respond.

"Do *you* think this work is sexist?" I asked. "Is asking a coworker to work on a PDF an act of exploitation now?"

"It doesn't matter what I think," Suzy replied. "You just need to treat Hazel like a friend."

"A friend? My 'friend' just complained that I am a sexist . . . what am I again?"

"An exploiter," Suzy said.

Then she became agitated. "I think you know what else she has accused people of. People have left the organization. I can't control what she does or says from here. You know she has quite an imagination."

My supervisor had just placed a gun to my head.

She ended the meeting with this final gem: "Unless you change your attitude, you're going to have to deal with the HR department and whatever happens. I don't know what to tell you."

At home that night, I stared at the dark ceiling above me, unable to sleep. Hazel is tough enough to manage, but how do I deal with Suzy?

This episode was one of a dozen times I was threatened via my supervisor because of, well, I have no idea. In the end (and every time thereafter), Suzy stopped just short of moving forward with a complaint. As correct a decision as that was, her inability to stop the cycle of silliness was almost as bad as having a complaint filed.

This is what a powerless manager dealing with a toxic employee looks like. Suzy's strategy was to do what she had to—*anything* to get through the day, week, or year—and last until she got her retirement package. It worked for her, but for everyone dealing with her and Hazel? Utter chaos.

And I wasn't the only person having to deal with Hazel. I was spending time every day dealing with Hazel's drama and kept thinking about how crazy it was to think it was cheaper to keep her.

What was the full price of dealing with the madness?

You're about to find out.

Chapter Ten

THE COSTS OF A TOXIC WORKPLACE

If you're a parent with children of a certain age, you have probably heard of FLARP. My daughter, despite being a girly girl, loved it when she was younger. FLARP is a disgusting, slimy, oozing, wet mound of putty you can buy at any toy store. You can shape it, twist it, roll it into a ball—and it horrifies any adult because of the cleanup involved with it. It's not only messy, but when you pull it out of its container, it sounds like flatulence. Add the feel and the sound together, and you have a kid's dream!

For toxic workplaces, when it comes to the well-being of companies and their workforce, FLARP is a nightmare. FLARP is my acronym that represents the many ways that toxic behaviors can affect an organization. Its effects can be just as messy to clean up as the putty but with a much bigger price tag.

FLARP has negative effects on

- Finances
- Legal matters
- Attraction and retention of employees
- Reputation
- Productivity and physical and psychological well-being

FINANCES

What happens to a company's bottom line if they hire a toxic person and leave them unchecked? Ask JPMorgan Chase. Bruno Iskil was a trader at JPMorgan Chase in London. He began aggressively trading in credit default swaps. They were noticed in his industry, earning him the nickname "Whale" and "Voldemort." Bruno and his boss, Achilles Macris, were known for throwing their weight around on conference calls and often shouting down colleagues in company meetings. It's classic toxic behavior and might even be addressed in some companies, except both Iskil and Macris made the company billions of dollars. They were untouchable.

When an employee knows they are untouchable, they often become overconfident and take risks they shouldn't. And why not? They know they won't get in trouble.

When Bruno's financial positions became targets for hedge funds, his aggressiveness blew up in his face. Initial losses on Bruno's transactions were over $2 billion, and future revisions put the total losses at over $6 billion. Investigations were launched, and the scandal soon reached across the entire organization, including CEO Jamie Dimon.

While Iskil did nothing illegal, his company suffered a number of financial blows:

- Two of the company's former traders (Iksil's former boss and a junior trader) faced criminal charges for attempting to hide losses from management.
- The company admitting to violating securities law.
- The company paid more than $1 billion in fines.
- The company paid more than $7 billion in legal fees.
- Dimon took a pay cut.[1]

By any definition, Iskil and Macris caused a lot of damage. There were systemic failures, particularly in the area of risk oversight, but it was the full-speed-ahead recklessness of this very toxic individual that lit the fire. JPMorgan Chase could literally have had billions of dollars more on its books if it had conducted the same oversight and had the same expectations it had for the rest of its major employees. They accepted the bad in order to cash in on the good. They lowered their standards. They should have checked their math. It wasn't cheaper to keep him.

Then there is the stomach-turning story of Hollywood power-player Harvey Weinstein's reign of terror via his role at the Weinstein Company. What was viewed by some investors as a firm with a $1 billion plus valuation at one time was sold for $289 million plus assumption of debt when Weinstein's disgusting acts drove down the value and reputation of the company. The winning bidder for Weinstein Company, Lantern Capital, set up a fund of $8.75 million to deal with pending lawsuits against the firm because of Weinstein's predatory actions. Harvey Weinstein and his brother Bob received nothing as a result of the purchase by Lantern. Toxic leaders and actions can obliterate a balance sheet.

Then there's absenteeism. Absenteeism is a purposeful and

intentional skipping of work because of conditions people are facing at the job. It's glorified hooky. It's a significant financial hit. And it's rampant in toxic workplaces because people have an oversized need to get out of the office.

How expensive is absenteeism? Kaiser Permanente analyzed employee absenteeism and estimated it costs businesses $1,685 per employee per year.[2] Workforce management consulting firm Circadian 24/7 Workforce Solutions puts the annual cost nationally at an average of $2,660 per person for salaried workers and $3,600 per person for hourly workers.[3] Overall, according to the Centers for Disease Control, employee absenteeism costs the entire United States economy $225.8 billion.[4] That's a lot of money!

And then there's the cost of dealing with a single toxic employee. Another study by Minor and Housman conducted at Harvard Business School looked at data on 50,000 workers from eleven different firms. It found that a toxic worker cost on average $12,489 to replace—and that doesn't include litigation, paying regulatory penalties, and a host of unquantifiable costs like low morale, loss of productivity, and good employees that leave as a result of the toxic employee.[5] The research further found that keeping out a toxic worker provides more than double the benefit of recruiting a single highly productive employee.[6] What's the key message here? You have more of an economic incentive with your hiring processes to aggressively keep toxic, destructive employees out than you do to search for the elusive superstar employee.

LEGAL ISSUES

The legal cost of the toxic workplace has two different columns: the public record showing legal actions filed due to hostile workplaces and the financial decisions made by companies because of legal concerns. Both are costly in their own ways. Lawsuits can destroy reputations and wreck finances. Paying money to settle problems caused by problem employees or the perverted management styles that emerge because of threats of lawsuits both have sky-high costs.

Lawsuits attacking the toxic workplace are traditionally filed based on unwelcome conduct or comments based on someone's gender, race, nationality, religion, disability, sexual orientation, age, or other protected class. According to the EEOC, "To be unlawful, [hostile] conduct must create a work environment that would be intimidating, hostile, or offensive to reasonable people. Offensive conduct may include, but is not limited to, offensive jokes, slurs, epithets or name calling, physical assaults or threats, intimidation, ridicule or mockery, insults or put-downs, offensive objects or pictures, and interference with work performance."[7]

As with sexual harassment suits, employers face legal exposure if they knew about harassment and did nothing or should have known and did nothing.

Some of these costs, especially during a time of high sensitivity regarding sexual harassment, are hitting employers where it hurts: the bank account.

In May 2017, two plaintiffs alleging their employer, Packer Engineering, ignored sexual harassment complaints, were awarded $6.45 million. Six million of the $6.45 million was punitive damages. The jury sought to punish Packer for their lack of action to protect employees.[8]

The US Supreme Court ruled in the 1990s that an employer is potentially liable when a supervisor creates a sexually hostile workplace environment.[9]

Do you have a harassment policy? Is it being enforced? If you're being lax on enforcement, watch out. If you think juries hit employers hard before for being soft on enforcing sexual harassment policies, just wait for #MeToo-era juries.

The taxpayers of Iowa had to pay $1.75 million to settle a sexual harassment-focused hostile workplace environment lawsuit filed by Kirsten Anderson, a former communications director for the Iowa Senate Republicans. Anderson had been fired by the Senate organization on the same day she submitted a memo detailing widespread sexual harassment at the state capitol. No doubt the Senate leadership thought she'd fold and go away. They were wrong.

Don't worry, my Democratic reader friends, not only could I have filled a couple of additional pages with other Republican sexual harassment scandals, but the Democratic Party is well-represented on this subject, too. Sleaze and dysfunction in the workplace and political arena seem to be the areas where both political sides can come together and agree to act badly.

What else can cost companies in dealing with toxic-workplace legal fallout? The discovery process. It can dig up unlimited problems. A cosmetics manufacturer was recently sued by a C-suite level employee for having a racially toxic environment. Does the lawsuit have merit? Only the legal process will determine if it does, but you can guarantee that the company will see its dirty laundry spread across the headlines for all the world to see.

Another lawsuit to watch is a November 2018 lawsuit against Lululemon, a Canadian athletic apparel maker. In the suit, a shareholder, David Shabbouei, claims that the actions of former CEO Laurent Potdevin were toxic, and the board of directors of Lululemon covered it up. The ensuing fireworks caused by that lawsuit should really be amazing.

ATTRACTION AND RETENTION OF EMPLOYEES

In even the best of economies, it can be difficult to retain good employees because organizations are paying top dollar as they expand.

Without a doubt, salary matters and pay raises will often cause an employee with a wandering eye to stay with their employer for the short term. However, a competitive salary mixed with a great culture is what causes great employees to stay for the long haul. In a 2017 study of 615,000 website users, Glassdoor found that the top predictor of workplace satisfaction is not pay. Rather, they found it is the culture and values of a company that brings the strongest satisfaction.[10]

Another big benefit is employees believing that their jobs give them purpose in life. According to a 2018 BetterUp Labs survey of nearly 2,300 American workers, nine out of ten employees said they would trade less money for a meaningful job. Professionals surveyed said that they would trade up to $21,000 in exchange for a job that is meaningful. Those surveyed were more likely to stay in a company longer and take fewer paid days off.[11]

To take the non-studied flipside of that for a moment, an employee whose life is spent meandering through arguments, division, and chaos is likely not to want to stick around as long; they will likely leave for a job that pays a little more and provides the proverbial bus ticket out of town.

While not studied by the Glassdoor work, imagine the impact of a toxic workplace culture on employees in a competitive job market! I won't reveal the firm's Glassdoor numbers, but you can correctly imagine how impactful they were for anyone with five minutes of time to read some reviews.

A March 2015 Cornerstone on Demand report, "Toxic Employees in the Workplace," found that employees are 54 percent more likely to quit when they work with a toxic employee.[12]

Losing employees costs a lot of money for retraining, depending upon the responsibilities. It robs the company of the talent and manpower needed to maintain high-quality operations. Institutional knowledge leaves as well.

REPUTATION

This is what is known as a target-rich environment. This chapter could be its own book. Where to start? With numerous CEOs forced to resign from organizations over a wide range of toxic workplace issues, it is clear that toxic workplaces can dramatically affect careers of all involved, no matter your perch or paycheck. Senior executives from Uber, Al Jazeera America, HTC, American Apparel, RAPP, the Humane Society of the United States, Hewlett Packard, Starwood Hotels, SoFi, and Ford Motor Company of North America are just a few examples of companies where leaders were forced out or reassigned in recent years because of their actions in creating or facilitating toxic workplaces. High-profile leaders may leave, but their bad behavior is often left to be cleaned up by the rest of the organization.

At Wells Fargo, a high-profile scandal involving bank sales-focused employees creating millions of fraudulent checking and savings accounts on behalf of customers without their consent, a toxic culture permeated throughout the organization. A lack of oversight and an aggressive, unchecked culture drove managers to encourage employees to create the fake accounts. When managers are systematically incentivizing their employees to engage in unethical practices across the organization, you have a heck of a problem—and a lot of people responsible. The illegal actions forced Wells Fargo to pay $185 million in fines and face numerous lawsuits. You would expect external lawsuits from shareholder groups in a scandal like this, but the company has also faced lawsuits from employees who say they were punished by managers for not creating fake accounts. You will see this frequently—in the midst of a toxic environment, it's not rare to see model employees punished, penalized, and put on the streets for doing the proper moral and ethical thing! In addition to the fines and the lawsuits, Wells Fargo's reputation has tanked.

With this toxic environment still in the news, Wells Fargo's once solid reputation has been destroyed. Shortly after the scandal broke in 2016, management consulting firm cg42 asked 1,500 bank customers about their perceptions. Some of the findings tell the story:

- Negative perceptions rose from 15 percent pre-scandal to 52 percent negative post-scandal.

- Positive perceptions went from 60 percent pre-scandal to 24 percent post-scandal.

- Over half of non-Wells Fargo customers said that they would be unlikely to do business with the bank.

- Only 3 percent of Wells Fargo customers were personally impacted by the scandal, but 30 percent said they were considering breaking ties with the bank.

- In 2017, the bank plummeted on the Harris Poll of Corporate Reputation from 70th in 2016 to 99th (out of 100), the biggest drop in the last twenty years of the poll.[13]

In the sports world, we recently saw the tragic story of the University of Maryland football team. Led by coach D. J. Durkin, an up-and-coming coaching star, Durkin and his staff led a purge of recruits that did not fit Durkin's mold. Many players left and others who did not get chased off were left to be humiliated by other coaches.

One player who remained on the team was Jordan McNair, a nineteen-year-old offensive lineman. After an excessively rigorous workout on May 29, 2018, McNair collapsed after running 110-yard wind sprints in scorching heat. McNair began showing outward signs of extreme exhaustion and an inability to stand upright. He soon collapsed, and normal instincts broke down. Despite trainers and other professionals with a strong understanding of McNair's medical problems—which included convulsions and a seizure—being on hand, team officials waited fifty-eight minutes to call 911.

Jordan was hospitalized and died two weeks later. According to an ESPN report, McNair died of heatstroke.[14]

Something troubling had happened, and news began to leak out. ESPN launched a full-scale investigative report, and the information was damning: Maryland's program had become the classic toxic workplace.

EPSN's findings included

- Fear and intimidation—Coaches had thrown weights and other objects at players.

- Belittling, humiliation, and harassment—A player coaches wanted to lose weight was ordered to eat candy bars in front of the team.

- Extreme verbal abuse—Players had their masculinity mocked when they could not complete a drill. A player who passed out during a drill was ridiculed in front of the team.

- In McNair's case, multiple sources told ESPN that as fellow teammates were literally holding McNair upright after he finished the last 110-yard sprint of his young life, a coach yelled, "Drag his ass across the field."[15]

Durkin and other coaches were initially suspended, a family's life was forever shattered, and inevitable legal actions by the McNair family and others were initiated.

And, of course, the reputation of the University of Maryland and its football program was justifiably tarnished. And then the school's Board of Regents made things even worse. They reinstated Durkin as head coach!

It only took a matter of hours for the public, major donors to the university, and Maryland politicians to weigh in and demand the regents reverse course. Durkin was fired. Decency was nowhere to be seen in the program, and the effort to rally around the toxic employees pointed toward a cultural problem far beyond the initial toxic behavior. They couldn't rationalize their decisions if forced to articulate them to anyone, but nevertheless they persisted out of a sense of preservation—self or otherwise.

Plenty of universities have their scandals—mine included—but the obvious signs of toxicity in the Maryland example, will hurt their program for a long time—and devastated a family forever. And the school's reputation? Likely tainted for a long time to come.

PRODUCTIVITY

Toxic influences can wreck an organization's productivity.

In their research paper "How, When, and Why Bad Apples Spoil the Barrel: Negative Group Members and Dysfunctional Groups," Will Felps, Terence Mitchell, and Eliza Byington found that a single negative employee can cause a 30 to 40 percent drop in a team's performance.[16] In a competitive business climate, this number alone is breathtaking in its potential damage.

Sherry, a non-profit executive in the Pacific Northwest, discussed the impact on her and her staff's time and productivity when her chamber of commerce elevated a highly disruptive, toxic individual to the chair role in the chamber of commerce she leads.

> My board of directors never asked questions about people who wanted to be on my board. We would take any warm body that showed an interest. Some of these "warm bodies" came with lots of baggage and had disrupted other organizations before—and my board knew it—but didn't want to stop it. A few years ago, the most toxic person in my community was added to the board. He was power hungry and divisive and immediately moved to get himself on track to join my executive committee. Once there, he was on the path to become chair.
>
> "No one thought he should be chair, but no one was willing to say that. No one. Board members resigned rather than fight. When he wasn't fighting with board members, he was causing fights around our community. We had members expressing concerns about whether the chamber was a place they wanted to invest their money. Leaders in the community said they would get back involved in the chamber once he stopped attending events. Since no other groups wanted him involved, we could not get rid of him. We were frozen in place. In a two-week span, seventy percent of my time was spent cleaning up problems he caused.
>
> "The entire year, we were less productive, our reputation worsened, and I avoided numerous projects because my chair would have been the face of them. It will take years for the scars to heal."

PSYCHOLOGICAL WELL-BEING

Toxic companies and employees steal the joy in an organization. The relationship between toxic organizations and their employees mirrors bad relationships.

Bullying, a common tactic to intimidate people in the toxic workplace, has been linked to complex post-traumatic stress disorder (C-PTSD). C-PTSD is an anxiety caused by long, multiple, and repeated trauma. Symptoms include irritability, reckless behavior, substance abuse, emotional numbness, memory problems, guilt issues, flashbacks, and lack of trust.

Along the same lines, a study by Dr. Alexander Tokarev of the University of Manchester (UK) Business School showed that employees who worked for bullies in the workplace had higher rates of depression and job dissatisfaction. Interestingly, the research also demonstrated that these affected workers managed by a bully with narcissistic or psychopathic tendencies showed a higher tendency to bully other people.[17] It's a vicious cycle.

Prominent therapists Dr. John Gottman and his wife Dr. Julie Schwartz Gottman have long prided themselves on an ability to watch two people in nonverbal communication—conversation on muted videotape, no audio—and predict in less than a minute, with near perfect accuracy, whether a marriage will survive or not. In other words, after six decades of practice, it is possible to spot the nonverbal signs of abusive behavior (even mildly abusive behavior).[18] Further, they have noted that victims of verbally abusive relationships get sick at a four times higher rate than national average. The reason for this is that psychological abuse literally weakens a person's immune system.[19] This can hold true for people who are involved in abusive psychological relationships in the office. Yes, you can be literally sick of your toxic coworker!

Another cost of toxic workplaces is seen when psychological abuse at work is carried back to the employee's home. An employee's worries don't end at 5:00 p.m. Those concerns are brought home and passed on in various ways to spouses and children.

PHYSICAL WELL-BEING

In his recent book *Dying for a Paycheck*, Stanford professor Jeffrey Pfeffer says that the workplace is the fifth leading cause of death in the US, ahead of Alzheimer's or kidney disease. Dr. Pfeffer's research estimates that 5 to 8 percent of healthcare costs and 120,000 deaths are due to mismanagement of the workforce. That mismanagement includes excessive hours, loss of control, work and family balance conflicts, and conflict in the workplace. Some of these issues are difficult to peg as due entirely to toxicity, but some factors can be lessened or largely eliminated as serious issues with better communication, support programs, and common-sense reforms to existing policies.[20]

Between 2008 and 2010, forty-six employees from France Telecom committed suicide during a time of layoffs and reorganization. Some of these employees undoubtedly committed suicide due to reasons well outside the control of France Telecom, but others left suicide notes specifically referencing issues at work.[21]

Additionally, a team of Swedish researchers at the Stress Institute in Stockholm conducted a survey of 3,000 men (aged nineteen to seventy) in a variety of work settings over a ten-year period. The researchers regularly asked those employees about their health problems as well as the personality characteristics possessed by their immediate superior. Their findings are eye-opening. Of the employees whose managers were described as *incompetent, inconsiderate, secretive,* and *uncommunicative,* a whopping 60 percent suffered heart attacks or other life-threatening cardiac conditions.[22] The research also found employees who described their managers positively were 40 percent less likely than normal to suffer from cardiac problems.[23] There was a clear inverse relationship between heart disease and the perceived *competency* of the manager. In other words, the more competent the manager, the lower the chance of heart disease. The more incompetent the manager, the better the chance of heart disease problems.

An October 2018 study by the University of Copenhagen, authored by Tianwei Xu and published in the *European Heart Journal,* tracked 80,000 workers in Sweden and Denmark for a significant period of time. None had history of cardiovascular disease going into the study. Nine percent of workers in the study identified themselves as being bullied by coworkers and 13 percent said they had been subject to violence or threats of violence in their workplace.[24]

The findings are stunning. Bullied workers had a 59 percent higher risk of cardiovascular disease. Those who faced violence or threats of violence had a 25 percent higher risk of cardiovascular disease. When frequency of threats, violence, or bullying was factored in, those who faced frequent, regular bullying or violence had a 120 percent higher risk level of cardiovascular problems.[25]

Despite all of this evidence, organizations vacillate every day about what to do with toxic employees. Whether it's out of the goodness of your heart or for your bottom line, employers, do you think it's time to take on the arsonists?

Chapter Eleven

FIREFIGHTING— CORRECTING AND REMOVING TOXIC EMPLOYEES IN A TOXIC WORKPLACE

I didn't realize it at the time, but when I joined the firm, it had already made a covenant with Hazel. When management signaled that no matter what she did, she would be protected, they created a code of conduct that literally had no rules—and the rest of the employee base knew it. Hazel became a protected class.

Toxic organizations getting rid of their arsonists is rare. In some cases, the arsonists may be the perfect cultural fit because the culture has been engineered to fit their needs.

Knowing this, if you are facing attacks from one of your toxic organization's arsonists, you need to be careful. You may be facing a battle you cannot win because the deck is intentionally stacked against you. As perverse as it sounds, arsonists may still be in their position for one of two main reasons—someone either wants them there because of their productivity, or someone is afraid to remove them because of obvious reasons or things you will never know. That "someone" is usually a person in power or a manager who cannot get rid of the employee no matter what.

The perceived irreplaceability of a productive employee can be overcome, but what about the other issues that engender fear in toxic management? Do you think your logical reasoning and well-documented evidence of corporate policies and norms can compete against the fear of what happens if previously threatened lawsuits, blackmail material, sticky personal relationships, corruption, and anything else that might concern toxic leaders were to surface? In toxic companies, many arsonists can become untouchable—immune from firing. They have a laminated, permanent "Get out of Jail Free" card.

You usually won't find out if someone is untouchable until you ask for your company to deal with them. I guarantee you will find out then, but likely not in a way you will like.

Babs Ryan, author of *America's Corporate Brain Drain,* says, "Only 1 percent of bullies are fired; action is usually taken against the [bully's] target. Your only choice may be to leave as quickly as possible—especially if the company supports that bully repeatedly and has already exited several of the bully's targets."[1]

One argument that employers sometimes make in defense of retaining high-performing toxic people is that these employees are "too important to lose." This could be true in isolated cases, but it's often not. Read on for research that spells out exactly that point.

More often it is a way for managers to avoid making hard decisions or may involve concerns about whether higher-ups will back them up. Or, in Suzy's case, she had been told her assigned arsonist was untouchable. What was she to do? She was risking her own job if she dropped the grenade she had been handed.

At some point, however, most companies need to get to the point of saying "Enough is enough!" and terminate the relationship.

But not every organization is ready to fireproof their organization immediately and get rid of their arsonists.

If they're not, a company's leadership need to look at themselves seriously and realize that their problem employees are actually calling the shots and controlling the culture, not the management. When that's the case, the employer is just as big a problem as the employee.

For managers wondering what to do with toxic employees, know that an organization has options. They aren't perfect fixes, but they can lead to changed behaviors if the company deals with the employee in a principled and firm manner. So, if needed, try these out if you think they will solve your problems. But, if you're dealing with an arsonist, these methods will be seen by them as a joke.

First, there are corrective measures.

Managers have a responsibility to correct toxic employees if they're being disruptive, of course. One method to deal with a toxic employee is to stage a series of workplace interventions, each more severe than the last.

This is known as the Disruptive Behavior Pyramid Intervention. It's a tool pioneered by Gerald Hickson, MD, a foremost expert on disruptive behavior.[2]

It consists of four steps, moving from the base of the pyramid to the peak.

First intervention—Put the concern on the record. There's a non-threatening drop-by type of feel to this step but one that should send a clear message. The discussion will usually be triggered by a first-time incident, and the discussion should be a private one without threats or warnings. The supervisor delivering the message will instruct the employee as to what is expected of them. The employee may grow defensive or try to minimize his or her actions, but the employer needs to be focused on action.[3]

Second intervention—Develop awareness. When step two occurs, it means that whatever happened to trigger the first intervention has continued. A major feature of the awareness step is that supervisors are supposed to show evidence or testimony documenting the employee's actions.[4] According to researchers at Vanderbilt University, the awareness step is very effective.[5] It's a "come to Jesus" type of moment, so to speak. It can be a time when even the arsonist knows they have been caught red-handed. It's where things get real in a hurry.

Third intervention—Exercise authority. When the first two steps don't work, it's time to kick it up a notch. This intervention is similar to step two but carries an accountability aspect as well. The supervisor lays out an improvement plan. The employee is told exactly what they need to do and what to expect if expectations are not met.[6]

Fourth intervention—Take disciplinary action. This is the last step in the process. If the employee fails to follow through with the system of accountability and goals involved in the third intervention, then the supervisor must take steps to punish the employee: reassignment, demotion, or termination.[7]

If you don't have the will to correct or terminate and somehow believe that the toxic employee's value is above having a highly functional workplace, there are other options. They don't eliminate the problem, but they can, if implemented, curb the growth of the problem.

The "bubble" is a way to let a company try to get the best of both worlds. It can also satisfy concerns from some legal departments about potential lawsuits from a termination.

With the bubble, you may have a high-value employee that, if they were not an abrasive jerk, would be a huge asset. Maybe they're brilliant, highly productive, or the son of the CEO.

How does it work? The organization blocks off or severely limits the toxic employee from supervising or interacting with other employees. By implementing the bubble, the company gets the work they want to receive from the toxic employee, limit collateral damage that can come with a high-value departure, and stops a damaging toxin from spreading. Win-win-win!

For the bubble to succeed, organizations need to be committed to enforcing it. Weak approaches make the situation worse. Toxic employees smell fear.

Isolation is a cousin to the bubble. In most companies I have interacted with, isolation tends to be connected to proximity. With isolation, the toxic person may move to a cubicle down the hall, but little else has changed. Teachers use this with regularity with children in their early years. In fact, I even used this method when I taught five-year-old children in Sunday school at my church.

One time, I moved a boy's chair to "time out" when his actions started to affect other kids. His sugar-high-induced antics were rubbing off. I placed his chair to face the window and told him that he could not play with any toys until he behaved. It took a whole thirty seconds before he started to pick up toys and launch them over his shoulder in the direction of the other kids. It was raining Hot Wheels and Tonka Trucks! I have to give the little guy credit though. He technically followed the rules about facing the wall. However, I failed to protect everyone else within the path of his torrential toy tossing. Why did I fail? My isolation really wasn't isolation, and I had no additional punishment to give out. And I knew his parents would pick him up in an hour. Even at his age, he likely realized that my "power" was going to end once his parents picked him up from the class and that there would be few consequences. It's no different with weak attempts to isolate a toxic employee.

A weak message can be worse than no punishment at all because it demonstrates that managers are impotent. Isolating problem employees a few desks away from other employees does nothing to solve the problem.

Another option for a manager having trouble getting buy-in for firing a toxic but high-performing individual is to "reward" them with the opportunity to work from home. Note that I didn't say this is a *good* option. Sure, the well-behaved employees catch a break from the arsonist in their office, but the worst offender in the office gets the perk of working from home? What an incredibly risky mixed message. But it can get the offending employee out of the office for a while and give management time to figure out what to do.

The tactics in this chapter will only work when a company shows they are serious. Arsonists know how to play the system and know if a company is serious. If there are not consequences, problems will only get worse.

As discussed elsewhere in this book, good employees can be flipped and become bad employees. It's the Tribble phenomenon.

Finally, if you are inventing new processes to fit individual employees, you may have lost the culture battle in your organization. You can't set policy based on exceptions to the rule, no matter how much you might want to avoid taking action or change the subject.

In conclusion, dealing with arsonists in the office is complicated, but it's not complex. Arsonists by every measure—legal, financial, productivity, retention, reputation, morale, and many more—are worth terminating. If they earn the title of arsonist through their actions, they have written their own script for being fired.

Look at the Top 20 signs of a toxic workplace earlier in this book. I can almost guarantee your company's arsonist is engaging in some, if not many, of these acts. As always, consult with an experienced employment law attorney before terminating any employee if a question about liability exists, but be bold and address your problem. It's simply *not* cheaper to keep them.

Chapter Twelve

ALICE IN WONDERLAND
AND THE FIERY FIRING

Incredible studies have been done about the effect of group think and mob mentalities. They have found that decent people can do incredibly destructive things if they feel pressure or self-interest to act like the rest of a group. I witnessed it. In acts to keep a toxic culture from destroying them—otherwise decent people did incredibly cruel and destructive things. And when the acts are to preserve themselves, they sometimes even do it with bravado—and, in this instance—nicknames.

Several months in, our administrative assistant Sarah, who jointly reported to both Hazel and me, left her position. I could not blame Sarah for leaving, not in the least. No amount of money was worth what she endured.

We needed a replacement—some poor soul who would be forced to deal with a job I would not have wished on my worst enemy. It is really the conundrum of working in a toxic workplace: no good person deserves to be brought in, yet nothing can change the dynamics if you don't have good people. With Suzy's approval, we held several rounds of interviews. Some included an HR presence in the meetings. Others had just Hazel and me in the room with the applicants. There began to be a certain three-step pattern with Hazel during the interviews.

1. We would ask questions and the applicants would respond.

2. We would thank them for coming, and they would thank us for having them.

3. The door would close behind the applicant, and Hazel would attack the wardrobe, looks, and morals of these complete strangers in their absence.

"Did she shop at Goodwill? She looked homeless!" Hazel would grouse.

"I couldn't look at that face for another second. Get her out!" That was another of her favorite lines.

At one point, Hazel even began to speculate about how many sex partners one candidate may have had: "She looks like a slut. Hundred-percent chance she's got a tramp stamp on her back. You don't have to share a toilet seat with that."

For me, the best comments involved Hazel speculating on whether someone might be toxic and difficult to work with.

The soon-to-be rejected applicants who were rejected did not realize it at the time, but a rejection email was the best news they could have ever received.

Finally, after lots of interviews with candidates, we found the impeccably qualified Barb. She was experienced and astute.

After a few weeks, Barb left and never was seen again. She was indeed astute.

So we posted the job again. We went through more interviews and more of Hazel's open-mic-night style belittling of each candidate.

Finally, we found someone that Hazel had not yet verbally ground into fine powder. This person was someone whom I was very happy to hire as well. As I think back, I don't know whether Hazel liked this woman for a fleeting moment or that she was too busy flinging poop at everyone else to focus on her. Either way, she slipped through the cracks and made the cut.

The new fodder for our most dysfunctional cannon was named Alice.

Alice was a nice woman, far too nice for this environment. With a great background and good references, I thought Alice could be someone who could elude some of the drama Hazel was known for. How I came up with that idea, I'll never know.

For a few months, Alice did well, and there were no problems in sight. She learned to master nearly everything that was put in front of her.

However, things turned on a dime with Hazel. Hazel began to utter strange notions about Alice's role, including the idea that she needed to do something to demonstrate her loyalty. I hadn't heard this schtick outside of Mafia movies. She verbalized at one point that "I want her to prove her loyalty. She should be willing to do anything I tell her to do. She's got to prove she wants to be on my team." Alice was a part of the team, but I think Hazel was meaning her own personal team.

Without any targets to immediately attack, Hazel sat in wait.

At the time this chapter's events began, I needed Alice's

help badly. I was entering a time when I would be traveling six days a week, sixteen to eighteen hours per day, crisscrossing the country to different state capitol buildings. I needed administrative support to help with my travel, scheduling my meetings, and doing basic research projects. I had no margin for error, which meant the interests of our clients did not, either.

Alice was a single mom who worked hard and took direction well. The only challenge Alice faced was a sporadic need to drive her elderly father to go to his doctor appointments. It was something that everyone knew about and agreed to when she was hired.

As someone who serves as a caretaker for my elderly mom, I was sympathetic to Alice's needs. If Alice came in a few minutes late in the morning or after lunch, she would leave a few minutes later in the afternoon. Problem solved, right?

Nope.

One day, Suzy walked by my office and said, "Come to my office in five minutes. We need to talk."

I made the trip down the hall by memory, my shoes having practically worn a path in the carpet by this point.

As I knocked on the door and entered, I could hear the soothing sounds of a mix tape of falling rain and chirping birds, but in a strangely high volume. Apparently, Suzy was feeling the need to reach some level of tranquility, and a monsoon with screeching birds hit the spot.

"Pete, would you like the music on or off?"

This is music?

"Maybe just a little less volume," I said, fearing a flock of birds would crash through a window at any moment in this torrential pseudo storm.

Despite the not-so-calm calmness, Suzy was, for once, projecting an outward appearance of serenity. Instead of her traditional six to eight stacks of folders, there was only one lone stack on her desk. What did all of this mean?

I sat down in the hot seat and waited for a shoe to drop. Or be thrown at me.

"Pete, you are a valuable part of our team."

I suddenly felt like the NFL coach who receives a public vote of confidence comment from the team owner during a losing season. What was this about?

"And I value you," I replied. OK, that felt a little awkward.

"We are needing to remove Alice from her position, and we need your support."

I sat up in my seat, my body language providing the initial rebuttal.

"You need to be a team player on this."

I was in a state of disbelief. "On what grounds?"

"We need to show a unified front," she said. "We need to agree here."

Note that there was no answer to my question, and Suzy was sounding like she was impersonating a secretary of state with the "unified front" talk. I continued pressing.

"Unified about *what*?" I said. "Do you have any grounds to fire this woman? Where is this idea coming from? And who's on this team?"

As Suzy finally answered, I noticed that she was trying to remain professional and composed. It was all in the eyes. "Hazel," she said slowly, "has complained that Alice's work is awful and that she is not fitting in."

And there it was. Hazel.

I shook my head no. "Alice's work is great, and she is fitting in very well."

"Not according to Hazel," said Suzy. "Alice has been out of

the office several times."

I reminded Suzy that arrival and departure times, as well as the occasional need to take her dad to a doctor's appointment, had been agreed to when she was hired. And, of course, there was my version of events regarding Alice's productivity and fit that was diametrically opposed to Hazel's.

But it was as if Suzy hadn't heard me or was holding another conversation entirely. "Pete, we need to make sure Hazel feels supported and that you are on board. This will be a good way to heal any hurt feelings between you."

Hazel, I apologize for you making up allegations against me, and sorry about the whole not reacting to the flashing the chest thing at the Chinese buffet. May I offer you a human sacrifice? I dreamed of saying as I mentally composed my healing, soothing words speech.

I could feel my blood pressure rising. Suzy was offering up Alice as a human sacrifice.

"I should help her get a good employee fired over things that were understood, discussed, and accepted by you and everyone else before she was hired. Does this even make sense to you?"

"It doesn't matter what makes sense to me. You need to be on board," said Suzy in a statement that I think probably sounded twisted even to her.

"Listen to what you just said, Suzy. You're better than this," I said.

At that point, I was starting to wonder whether she was better, but I didn't have lots of other options.

I left her office, disgusted by what I had just heard.

This deck was stacked.

A few days passed, and the *Fire Alice!* baton was handed over to the HR department. In most cases, that would be good news, as healthy HR departments would usually do their digging and discover the flimsy accusations for what they were.

But HR departments serve as a reflection of the organization's management style. They can be ethical and "by the books," or they can be used to protect certain management within the company at all costs. I was about to find out what type of HR department I was working with.

Human resources was led by HR Harry. Harry was slick, not substantial. His hair spiked high and his suit material often strangely glistening, he was more politician than manager. His rapid-fire speech reminded me of a shell-game-playing New York City street hustler—talking fast, moving pieces around, and putting people on the spot to make fast decisions. He was a deal-cutting, friend-protecting, bullet-dodging, chainsaw-juggling, policy-morphing whirling dervish of a man. "By the books" meant works of fiction. Confidential meetings may as well have been press conferences.

On a Friday afternoon, Harry popped his head into my office and asked me to call him the next morning, a Saturday. He didn't say what he wanted to talk about, but it was easy to guess.

The next morning, I made the call. With coffee in hand and dressed in my traditional Saturday uniform of shorts and a T-shirt, I sat by my pool and began to feel the machinations of a spin doctor over the line.

"Pistol Pete, my friend," came his rapid-fire, game-show-host sounding voice. "How are you?" Harry referred to me as "my friend" a lot. So much that the overuse of it had started to make me wonder whether he was overcompensating. The "Pistol Pete" thing was new—it was minted that very morning.

"A weekend call, Harry? What's this about?" I said.

"Well, it's about Hazel and Alice."

"Really? I'm shocked," I deadpanned.

"What do you think about Hazel's comments?"

"Alice is a great employee. These are lies."

I heard Harry sigh on the other end of the line. "But there's lots going on here. You need to understand everything in play."

"And she's dealing with a sick, elderly parent. And I told you personally when she was hired that she would need to go to an occasional doctor's appointment, and you agreed to it, Harry."

"That may be, but things change, Pistol Pete. The world changes. We didn't have cell phones thirty years ago. And a reprimand is really not enough, the more I talk to you. We need to give Hazel a win."

"On what grounds?" I said. "And why are we talking about wins?"

"Pistol Pete, help me out with Hazel here," he replied. "Besides, we both know this is more about you than Alice. You can win here, too, if you're strategic."

I had to unpack that comment in my mind for a moment. It wouldn't come out. "Harry, what do you mean that you need to help Hazel?

"Look, I have a few problematic little HR issues that Hazel had reminded me of." He cleared his throat. "You know how it is." He giggled. "You know how it is."

I actually didn't know how it was—not at all. But the next thing I knew, he was explaining "how it was" to me.

Good Lord, I thought. How bad have things become in the culture when the HR department needs an HR department?

"Look, I'll be honest with you," Harry said, with all the authenticity of a seven-dollar bill.

"You weren't before?" I said with a smile. "I'm kidding." All right, no, I *wasn't* kidding.

"Alice's performance is not the issue. Her real problem is that she is expendable because of the big picture."

"I'm not surprised, Harry." In fact, I was surprised—and nauseated.

Next, he cleared up what I had wondered about—that is, the real reason for Alice being on the hot seat was about me. In Hazel's twisted thinking, firing Alice would load hours and hours of extra work onto my back.

Harry put a fine point on it: "She wants to weaken you when you can least afford for it to happen. She's good!"

It was breathtaking. The human resources leader was complimenting the attack on other employees like he was watching a tennis match. It was disheartening, even by the firm's standards.

Just days after the call with Harry, he stopped by my office seconds after I had come to work. He said, "Knock, knock, Pistol Pete. You don't look busy. Can I come in?" as he walked in and closed the door. He strolled over to my desk and handed me a short document.

"What's this?" I said.

"Read it," said Harry

I looked through it while he stood there, standing over me. He was close enough to me that I could hear him breathing. It was an evaluation of Alice's performance, and it had been written by Hazel. Filled with fabrications and distortions, the only things Alice had not been blamed for were global warming and the Kennedy assassination.

"This is ridiculous," I said.

"Sign it," he replied.

I looked up at him. "No. Impossible. This is a nonstarter. Did you even read this?"

Harry moved alongside me at my desk and placed his hand

on my shoulder muscles and began squeezing them like he was a boxing manager trying to coax a fighter back into the ring. "You *have* to, Pistol Pete. Or I can't protect you either," he said.

"No." I paused briefly. "Wait, protect *me*?"

"Just sign it."

"You're messing with a woman's life to protect yourself. I am not signing this," I said.

"You need to do something or we're both going to have problems," he replied.

"That something is helping to get Alice fired because Hazel is creating problems for you. What does she have on you?" I said.

For once, Harry had nothing to say.

I put the paper down on my desk and waved to it to indicate that he could pick it up if he chose to. Angry at my refusal, he snatched it up and stormed out.

For days, I was pained at the thought of how this entire scenario would play out. While I had blocked action temporarily, Harry wasn't going to stop things completely.

Later, however, Harry called me on the phone. "Pistol Pete, it's Harry."

Again with the Pistol Pete.

"I wanted to let you know that we have created an improvement plan for Alice."

"An improvement plan?"

"That's right."

"I was not involved in creating an improvement plan for Alice. I'm her supervisor."

"No need," he said smoothly. "Now, you have two options. One, sign the document, and Alice stays. Two, don't sign the document, and Alice is out by lunch because of what I have on paper already."

"Some choice, Harry. I thought our goal was improvement. If I don't sign something, she is fired? What does my action have to do with Alice's improvement?" I said.

"Mom gave us one choice at dinnertime. Sometimes you don't get to choose. I'll send it over to you. I want an answer by the end of the day."

Minutes later, the plan popped up in my inbox. This was a firing plan, not an improvement plan. Most companies use improvement plans legitimately. Some play games with them. It included a provision that called for immediate termination if Alice arrived late or left early at any time. To enforce this, HR was going to check her entrances and exits via the data on her employee badge.

Traffic, a car breaking down, her watch a minute off, or anything else could trigger Alice being fired. It was like strapping a bomb to someone and telling them they'll live as long as they never move.

There was not a single person in the firm that would remain employed under this standard. Heck, Harry was rarely on time himself, but fairness wasn't a consideration here.

I faced a choice and, regrettably, I signed the document. It wasn't a question of if Alice would be forced out, but when and how.

I wasn't wrong with my assessment, but what I didn't know is that things would get even worse.

Harry arranged a meeting with Alice, Hazel, and others to discuss her improvement. It had all the feel and legitimacy of a show trial that you might see in a third-rate dictatorship. Allegations, finger-pointing, and foolishness abounded.

At that point, Hazel decided that it was open season on poor Alice's morale.

Hazel began imitating Alice's low voice and her walk—all

just steps away from Alice's desk. Then she started making snide remarks as soon as Alice arrived each day. "God, when will I get some decent help?" she would mutter from her desk to no one in particular but targeted for Alice's nearby ears. She took every opportunity to belittle the woman. It was cruel and constant.

As Hazel's pile-on continued, I pulled Alice aside one day when I noticed the stress particularly overwhelming her.

"Look," I said, "you shouldn't have to go through this."

"Thank you," she mumbled. I could see that she was the type of person who was maintaining grace in the most classless of environments.

"This is not your fault. We're dealing with some really devious people."

"Oh no, I would never say that," she said.

Alice, both to her credit and detriment, had a good heart.

"Then I will, Alice. Let me give you some advice. If you want to stay here, don't let Hazel see that she's getting to you," I said. "It will only get worse."

"OK," she said sheepishly.

"I will do everything I can."

As my mouth said those words, my heart knew something far different. Alice did not have a prayer of staying in the job. I was trying to be encouraging, but my words were hollow. I had no idea how to help this poor woman.

As time went on, Alice's will to continue diminished daily, and the emotional gauntlet she was facing was taking a toll. Her body language spoke in ways that words never could. She grew physically smaller, her shoulders hunched and her head tipped down toward her chest as she walked. When Hazel was near, Alice would literally lean away. How could she be expected to perform when she knew she could be fired at any moment?

She couldn't. I knew this charade would come to an end soon.

One day, Alice's father had a vital medical appointment that she absolutely had to attend. She was the driver, and he had been having a rough couple of weeks. These appointments can always run longer than expected, as we all know what doctor's offices are like during flu season. Hazel pounced on the departure, and I knew what to expect next. Hazel contacted both Harry and Suzy. They said that Alice would be fired immediately.

I called Alice, and she picked up quickly.

"Alice, it's Pete."

"Hi Pete, I'm gonna be back at any minute, I just had to—"

"Don't come back," I told her. "I don't know how to say this. Just don't come back."

"Why? I'm almost there."

"They're going to fire you. Don't come back. I'm so sorry." I could hear Alice sobbing on the other end.

We hung up, and I felt a little relieved. While I did not want to see her leave, and a part of me wanted to see her fight, Alice did not need to be humiliated one last time. Later that afternoon, an HR representative called her and informed her of her termination.

I closed my door for the day and wondered what level of hell is reserved for people who treat the vulnerable in the way Alice had been treated. And I thought about what I could have done to protect Alice. Given the corruption of standard processes, the answer may have been nothing, but that gave me no solace.

Two weeks after Alice was fired, I received an email from her.

"Pete, I wanted to let you know that my dad passed away peacefully yesterday morning. He gave it all he could. Thanks for supporting me when I needed it. I don't have money or a job, but I got to have extra time with him. Thanks for all you did."

Ever the optimist, Alice had turned a nightmare into a positive. The speedy termination, as painful as it was, was better than a prolonged, torturous firing, and she got to be there for her father's final days.

If an organization was a human body, the HR department would be the kidney—a vital organ that keeps things clean. Remove the kidneys and the body will break down over time.

HR is supposed to oversee orderly processes of management, not facilitate shams. If that department is corrupted by agendas, the rest of the organization will suffer.

C-suite leaders, what types of decisions are your managers rolling the dice on because they are forced to keep the arsonists around the organization?

In closing out this chapter, I leave you with a point of personal privilege. In preparing this book, I reached out to Alice to see if I could tell her story. She assured me I could.

The Alices of the office are affected every day by bullies and agendas within the toxic workplace. They're nameless, faceless people who are collateral damage for those who look at bigger pictures or turn their heads to look at different pictures entirely. They don't have the trappings of power, the levers to pull, or the dirt to spread. They're simply individuals caught up in games they didn't even know they were playing.

While this book is for everyone at organizations, I hope the positive impact of fireproofing organizations is felt first by the Alices of the world. If it helps them, I will have done some good. Not one more person should be driven out of a job because managers simply abdicate their responsibilities.

Chapter Thirteen

HR IN TOXIC ORGANIZATIONS— POURING GASOLINE ON THE FIRE?

You just read what can happen when an HR department loses its way—or more appropriately, is perverted from any reasonable definition of what their role is supposed to be.

I have worked with numerous great HR departments and one that was corrupted beyond recognition.

HR departments reflect the top of the organization. In healthy organizations, that means the HR department joins with the company's top leaders to help the enterprise soar to new heights. In toxic organizations, HR departments can help guide a company and its employees over a cliff in a number of different ways.

This chapter is not a "bash HR" rant. Far from it. In fact,

many items within this chapter and throughout this book have been strengthened by leaders within the HR world. HR departments can do great things—if they're empowered to do so. Or they can do some not so great things if they're *forced* to do so. Especially if those things defy what a good HR function is supposed to do. Cultures and ethics matter, and people in HR departments are as affected by those things as much as anyone. We're all human.

This book deals with toxic workplaces, and this chapter focuses on toxic HR departments. Nothing in this chapter, other than the basic descriptions of what traditional HR departments do and don't do, deals with the way most companies or all HR departments operate. I am talking about what can happen if HR departments are forced to be part of a toxic team and the ability they have to spread toxicity like wildfire. As with any other high-pressure, unethical culture, normally good people can do some very destructive things. And some very destructive people, if placed in HR departments, can make their profession look bad.

Human resources departments are badly misunderstood and usually underutilized for the expertise they bring to personnel decisions and their understanding of workplace dynamics.

HR departments can greatly benefit all employees if they have a seat at the table when decisions are made. Or, as they are in many toxic companies, they sometimes are stuck watching from the sidelines when decisions are made and are brought in at the last minute to implement some very bad ideas.

No matter what type of culture you are in, the purpose of an HR department is not to protect you as an individual employee. I repeat, HR is not there to protect you. Instead, HR is there to serve a company's goals as defined by management in a variety of ways, including processing payroll, hiring and firing, benefits, and keeping a company in compliance with federal state and local laws. Perhaps most importantly for those dealing with a toxic environment, HR plays a major role in minimizing legal and financial liability concerning any personnel matters.

What is *not* included in that list?

- HR is not your priest, your buddy, or your lawyer. They are not required to keep discussions confidential. If you don't want your thoughts—no matter how legitimate they are—discussed with your entire executive team, it may be best to keep quiet until you have a better idea of what will happen if you speak up. Brainstorm with a trusted friend inside the company who understands how complaints are handled. If you are talking about personnel issues, personal issues, or ethical issues, watch out. If the matter is serious enough, talk to an employment attorney for advice. Just know that if you talk with HR, the person who is causing you problems may soon know exactly what you said. Tread carefully.

- HR will not necessarily be your champion even if you're a good person, a great employee, dead-on right when it comes to company policy, or the only ethically correct person in the dispute. They might root for you personally, but that will be immaterial if helping you means pulling off a scab that will embarrass the company, cause them a lawsuit from an erratic and volatile employee, or hurt the friend or ally of someone in management. If you are in a toxic company and your situation is volatile, talk to HR only if you are prepared to potentially lose your job as a result or have absolute 100 percent certainty of the results.

- HR does not dictate how upper management operates. In fact, HR is unfortunately not in the room when some companies make major decisions.

- HR knows things you don't, and they don't have to tell you what those things are. Know this: HR knows which employees are viewed as untouchable—meaning they likely can't be fired. You, on the other hand, may not fall into that protected class. Clashing with an untouchable may prove it.

As we learn at various times in life, good people end up doing bad, uncharacteristic things because of the environment they are in—often because of a desire for self-preservation. HR departments in toxic workplaces are no different and can often serve as an accelerant for the fires arsonists in the office have started.

Signs that an HR department is accelerating a toxic work environment include any of the following:

- Goal posts move. HR has different procedures, depending on people and situations. Alice's nightmare scenario is a perfect example.

- HR people tend to find fault, looking for ways to officially write up concerned employees for tiny infractions. This is often a protective action by the company in preparation for possible legal maneuvering.

- HR representatives begin to play detective or begin asking about a situation preemptively.

- HR staff watch incompetent or toxic people get promoted. This occurs often because following directions trumps other standard HR practices. HR leaders want to please current management, and if a toxic employee gets dirt on top management or HR leaders, that person will stay protected in the company for a long time.

- Good employees disappear. Remember so-and-so who was doing well but had that one concern about what was happening in accounting or had a problem with how his employees were being treated by one of the top executives? They may have left on their own, or they may have been the victim of a precision attack on their employment.

The common denominator in all of these issues is an HR department that operates outside of standard norms. HR departments in healthy cultures recognize an ounce of prevention is worth a pound of cure, that taking care in hiring and employee retention will greatly reduce the number of potential lawsuits and embarrassing issues that could attract media attention. If, however, HR staff is doing the bidding of toxic decision-makers, all bets are off.

Ethically challenged HR departments in toxic organizations can make existing problems worse or, other times, start to create their own problems.

In 2017, Wynn Resorts founder Steve Wynn was ousted from his casino empire after a flood of sexual harassment scandals. It was soon discovered that his biggest enabler had been his HR head. One spa attendant, Angela Saxton, who claimed she was sexually assaulted by Wynn in the early 1990s, said that she was later accosted by Arte Nathan, the head of human resources at the time. "You need to keep your mouth shut," he reportedly told her.[1]

The reason for all this toxicity? Not surprisingly, money and sex, or maybe sex *then* money. In fact, when Wynn was coming under fire and before he stepped down, his company put out a howling protest of a press release. It noted that Steve

Wynn owned 12 percent of the Wynn organization, and that "if we lose the services of Mr. Wynn, or if he is unable to devote sufficient attention to our operations for any reason, our business may be significantly impaired."[2] It reads like Wynn wrote it himself.

Just as appalling is the role of HR in this saga. They didn't do their job, not by a long shot.

As you consider the Wynn example, think of the chilling message sent to employees when they realized that the referees on company policies and personnel are serving as the palace guard for the CEO's sexual mores.

Just as interesting are the scandals created by HR departments themselves. You'd think HR departments might be immune to the bad behavior exhibited by other departments since they're the ones responsible for policing it. However, the problems continue.

For instance, in 2009, the employee relations director for the City of Nashville and Davidson County, Tennessee, was accused of sexual harassment by female members of his staff. A female payroll coordinator provided evidence and testimony during the internal investigation about the director's behavior, but she did not file a harassment claim. After the city investigated, the director was not disciplined, and the payroll coordinator was fired. She immediately filed a lawsuit claiming retaliation. But because she had not previously filed a harassment claim, the lower court found that the law did not protect her from retaliation.

The case went to the US Supreme Court, which ruled in *Crawford v. Nashville,* that the employee *could* claim she was fired in retaliation even without formally filing a complaint.[3] The case was sent back to the lower court, and a jury awarded the employee $1.5 million in compensatory damages, back pay, and future lost wages.

Then we have the example of the multi-year example of Corey Coleman, the now-former human capital officer of the Federal Emergency Management Agency (FEMA). In his role, which spanned multiple presidential administrations, Coleman allegedly transferred women to various departments, so his friends could try to have sexual relationships with them, according to the *Washington Post*.[4] Additionally, an internal investigation found that Coleman engaged in a sexual relationship with a subordinate and denied the woman a promotion when she began to refuse his advances.

An investigation into a *second* sexual relationship with a different subordinate found Coleman instructed a woman to work from his home and to accompany him on business trips. When she wanted to leave FEMA, Coleman created a new job for her as an enticement to stay in the agency. Coleman did not have a budget for this newly created job, so he utilized—wait for it—disaster response funding to finance her role. How appropriate!

Remember the old Greek saying: A fish rots from the head.

That can apply to heads of corporations or single departments. Or, in the case of Nashville and FEMA, governmental entities.

If you have a problem within your company and your HR department appears to operate similar to any of the situations I have listed above, watch your back if you want to keep your job. Read ahead about my thoughts on whether to speak up or not about problems in the workplace. The job you save may be your own.

Now let's talk about what an HR leader should look like in a modern organization. They should not be the gossiper-in-chief or the hatchet man trading personnel decisions for favors. They should be a major part of improving and leading the organization.

I have encountered too many organizations where HR is not a key player in making decisions. Sometimes they are among the last to know but are then asked to implement the decisions.

Thankfully, that is changing as companies realize that personnel decisions truly dictate performance and productivity.

For organizations to succeed, their HR leadership must succeed. That means hiring a high-level person of impeccable character and boldness, someone who is comfortable at the table with the rest of the C-suite or will very comfortably grow into that role.

An HR leader needs to be someone who, with their strong ethical compass, will not bury problems, but help solve them. That person also needs someone who can look at the big picture laid out by top leadership and be ready to make bold decisions to prepare the company for the future—that means they'll be asking for and ready to protect the necessary funding to attract, train, and develop employees at all levels.

An HR leader should be someone who can partner with departments to identify the best talent.

An HR leader also needs to be someone with the gravitas to identify issues and address them. Some of those may be personnel issues. Others, especially in fast-growing companies, may be tied to the lack of training that managers receive. Companies that are enjoying spectacular growth are promoting good people to higher levels in organizations but are not requiring or providing the most basic training in what responsible management looks like. That needs to change, as it's not fair to the untrained managers or the employees being managed.

Imagine the positive results when organizations move their HR departments to not only process issues but also truly become innovators and people who empower within organizations.

What does all of this vision lead to? An HR department that is at the table when key discussions are made and treated as a respected partner throughout the organization. That vision of HR is where organizations need to go to compete in the long run.

C-suite leaders, have you thought about the role of your HR department? Do you have the right team? Are you giving them what they need? Are they serving the right role? Do you have HR leaders at the table when you're making decisions? If not, why not?

Chapter Fourteen

PEAT AND REPEAT

There's a thing called peat. It's decayed material in the earth that can keep a wildfire alive even though the outward signs at any given time indicate that the fire has died down or been extinguished. The fire has gone underground. It's there, but you don't see it. As long as there's fuel and oxygen, the fire will continue to burn and emerge again at unexpected times.

An arsonist's fires only need a few key elements, too. But sometimes they go underground. And then they reappear. Hazel's actions would rest, but they would never stop. I don't believe her internal makeup allowed it. When she lacked a specific target, her behaviors just went underground and built up enough oxygen and fuel to come back to life when the opportunity presented itself. The fires often involved me, but more often she focused on those around me or moved slowly, causing trouble and discord in small ways.

Alice was not the only one that was attacked for their connection to me—however tangential—within the organization.

In fact, with as many stories as people shared with me, it appeared easier at times to remember the short list of those whom had not been on Hazel's hit list than the long list of people who had.

Meet Jen.

Universally held in high regard, Jen was one of the hardest-working employees the firm had. We were friends because of her continuous but fun-loving mockery of my alma mater. Jen was a nose-to-the-grindstone type of employee—a hard worker who did her work and always accentuated the positive. At the time she was also looking for an opportunity to move up in the organization and make more money. With three teenagers, she had college to pay for.

One day, Jen applied for a job with a department within the firm not directly connected to mine.

Then the attacks began.

Jen came to my office one day. "Pete, do you have a minute?"

"Sure," I said. In truth, I didn't, but she looked ill. As she usually had perpetual smile on her face, I knew something was up.

Walls had ears in the building, so in a show of good judgment, she waved me out of the office and then to the middle of the parking lot. It was as though Jen thought the building was under surveillance!

She began distractedly tracing lines on her chin with her fingertips and adjusting her bangs to get them away from her eyes. Jen looked really nervous.

"What's up?" I said.

It took her a minute to answer. "You know the hiring manager over in the research department, Albert?"

I nodded. "I don't know him well, but yeah, I know him."

"He just told me that Hazel has been contacting him every day about me."

"What is she saying?" I said.

"She's been feeding him negative stories about me, telling him why I shouldn't be hired."

"She barely knows you. Why would she do this? " I said, right as my thoughts collided with the obvious reason Jen would soon deliver.

"Pete, think about it. We're friends."

I doubled over, disgusted but not surprised. "I can't believe this," I said, fully knowing that this was entirely believable.

"Hazel is famous for things like this. She does whatever she thinks will get attention," said Jen.

Jen was one of many people who would face the wrath of Hazel as soon as she realized I was connected to them in any way.

Kara was another. She was a longtime friend of mine, and in a group conversation one day, with Hazel present in the room, I mentioned that Kara was a friend for whom I had a great deal of respect.

Within days, Hazel was on the attack, bashing Kara to anyone that would listen with some incredibly personal attacks. And they did not even know one another! Kara got wind of Hazel's comments and asked why my colleague was talking about her. I had no response but to apologize. There was literally no rational explanation.

This was just one more effort to create drama and disruption and to make sure I would hear about it.

At least within the firm, Preston was at the head of the line when it came to Hazel's victims. While someone somewhere likely had faced her wrath pre-firm, he got the brunt of her 2 x 4 wielding right off the bat within that organization.

Preston should have been Hazel's favorite. He hired Hazel just before he left on a brief sabbatical to study philosophy in the Himalayas. Preston graciously told Hazel to use his office in his absence. It was located close to other key employees, and Preston thought that would get Hazel acclimated quickly. And it did, but not in the way he expected.

Minutes after Preston departed for the Himalayas, Hazel's first move was to call the maintenance department to remove Preston's name plate from the office door and replace it with her own! Can you almost hear the electric screwdriver now?! The metaphorical moving truck backing up to help replace his career with hers? When Preston finally returned, he came back to a workplace that was barely recognizable. One meeting after another took place during the sabbatical time where Hazel sowed doubt, division, and disinformation about Preston—a man she somehow thought stood in her way at the firm. People had allowed Hazel's lies to fill the vacuum. He left the firm a few months later when he realized that the job had become intolerable. He had literally let the arsonist into his office. He could have fought battles with Hazel and tried to fire her for insubordination, but he did not have the stomach to stoop to Hazel's level. Out went a good employee, along with an incredible institutional history, and in came the arsonist.

This is precisely the type of cost that is never calculated when employers consider whether to deal with the arsonist employee or not.

Preston's experience was notable for another reason. He learned that Hazel had no fear of repercussion for her actions and thought nothing of saying whatever it took to attack someone's reputation. Sadly, that lack of caring about consequences works exceptionally well for arsonists. Lies expertly fill a vacuum, and my political experience informs my belief that personal or professional attacks should never be ignored. If you're under attack, you must respond. If you don't, you can expect more attacks. There's a reason why negative political ads work. It's the old saying of "If you say something often enough, people will believe it." Preston didn't even know what hit him, never responded, and found himself bolting from his job just months after Hazel started. He was disgusted and fled. The result in this match? Hazel in a knockout.

Lupe pulled me aside in the halls of the firm one day to share her concern for my professional well-being. Instances of conversations with people like her were one of the most unusual things about my time at the firm. People approached me at times like we were meeting in a dark alley. I had never met her, but those with Hazel horror stories were everywhere. She recounted a story of shocked and horrified coworkers who dared disagree with Hazel. When someone suggested a different idea about how to tackle a problem the firm faced, Hazel filed frivolous hostile workplace complaints against not one, but eight people! If it was laughed off, that would be one thing. However, a paralyzed organization treated Hazel's complaint like it was Moses delivering the Ten Commandments. Every one of those employees was run through a ridiculous process that determined that, *gasp*, employees disagreed with Hazel.

Then there was Brad. A mutual friend connected us, so I could hear and learn from his story. When he asked me naively if anyone else had talked to me about Hazel, I had to tell him that he was one of dozens who came to me to tell me their cautionary tales. I think that in some way that made him feel better. We met for lunch, and it took only seconds before he jumped into action. He had a story to tell.

"I never said a word to Hazel about anything other than business," he said, his voice breaking. "She was a colleague and seemed like a friend. Then, out of nowhere, she filed a sexual harassment complaint. I told my wife I didn't do anything wrong, but she hasn't looked at me the same way since. She doesn't trust me. She thinks no one would file a complaint if nothing had happened. The firm treated me like I was a criminal, and I had literally never said a thing to Hazel outside of meetings."

Brad was devastated by the experience and left the firm shortly after our lunch. His employer had allowed him to be treated like a gun-range silhouette, and he knew the firm would do nothing to deal with one of Hazel's frivolous complaints. Who could blame him?

I never knew where the attacks would come from next and, obviously, neither did anyone else.

Sometimes Hazel's tool was sabotage. A couple of times, it involved a PowerPoint presentation I was giving. There I would be in front of an audience, and a slide would pop up that I had never seen before. And my tap dancing at that point would show just how surprised I was because I had to then explain what was on the slide—while looking at it for the first time. Incensed, I would go immediately to Suzy but was told how important it was to be "on my toes." On your toes doesn't translate into "expect your work to be sabotaged by a coworker." But at the firm, it always did.

Other times, I didn't know if I was dealing with bad behavior or something beyond it—a disconnect of sorts that was not run-of-the-mill toxic behavior.

Generally speaking, Hazel had gotten her wings clipped by the organization for unnamed problematic behavior. Her role had been reduced. That was stated to me in a number of ways and times, but they held back in curtailing other areas in the spirit of "it's cheaper to keep her" or "don't poke the bear" or whatever was the band-aid-driven slogan of the day.

They clearly were in fear of Hazel, but they also coddled and played games of pretend as a way to deal with the problems.

As a result, the firm's treatment of Hazel took on the feel of talking with my sweet Irish grandma when she was in her nineties. Grandma had her own reality at that point. I saw her one time, and she didn't know who I was. We began talking about other people in my family, and she chimed in with, "What's Little Pete doing these days?" Despite pulling out my driver's license and explaining that I was actually the Little Pete she was talking about, she was in her own reality. At her age, that was A-OK. We just worked with whatever reality was in her mind. It was harmless.

The coddling of Hazel went similarly, but it presented high-risk problems. And it wasn't harmless. And Hazel sure wasn't ninety.

Hazel's responsibilities had been changed significantly upon my arrival, which would normally be followed by a change in title to accurately reflect the new responsibilities or at least differentiate it from the new position. But in negotiations between Hazel and her superiors, a concession was made to not change her title. I knew this had been a sticking point because Suzy had pointedly told me early on that discussing the changes in roles with anyone outside the organization would be viewed as rubbing salt in Hazel's wounds and was prohibited. How convenient.

The unchanged title became a way for Hazel to have unlimited opportunities to muddy waters, blur lines, and throw bombs.

Thus, we had two people working in my job. One was me, the person actually assigned to speak on behalf of the organization to legislators and members of Congress in key states.

The other was a person with the right title on a business card but no standing other than that given by a lack of action on the part of her supervisors and an unlimited penchant for mischief. But, as with my earlier reference to Frank Abagnale in *Catch Me if You Can*, it's amazing what damage can be done if an employee has no fear of consequences if they're caught.

In a legislative environment, having two negotiators—especially one who is real and the other imagined—is about as helpful as having two different bomb squad members, each guessing which is the correct wire to cut to prevent a bomb from detonating.

After a dicey episode in which Hazel and one of her colleagues began speaking for the firm in a way that risked blowback and burned relationships, I reached out to Suzy.

"Suzy, we've got a problem. I'm here in Virginia, and Hazel is talking with the Agriculture Committee members as though our firm and our client supports an amendment affecting the cashew farmers. In fact, they don't. I've had five legislators complain that we are taking this position, which was surprising to me because, we are *not!*"

I could visualize Suzy making her way into an underground bunker.

"I don't know that I can talk with her about this, Pete," she said.

"But you're her supervisor, right?" I coached.

"I would rather not discuss this with her," she said, volleying the ball well into somebody else's court.

Another time, the firm had helped a very important client file some state-level legislation on an issue in Montana.

Hazel had qualms about the bill but outright spite for the person who would be delivering the message on this legislation. It was a pattern—her occasional opinion on an issue was not always out of line, but the behavior was another story. And that productivity might be secondary to attacking someone on her hit list.

After the bill was filed, supporters held a press conference in the rotunda of the state capitol in Helena, a beautiful room adorned with pictures of Montana's historic leaders.

Representing the firm and our clients that day was noted fish expert Grace, a consultant on all underwater matters. I tagged along, as I never missed out on a trip to Montana. No serious opposition had emerged, so I believed we had smooth sailing ahead.

The bill dealt with a change to the law that signified the spotted cutthroat trout as Montana's official state fish. The full language in state law would state in perpetuity that, despite the fish's name that included the word "cutthroat," the creature was not violent and was, in fact, a kind and peace-loving fish.

The press conference began right on time, and Grace delivered an excruciatingly detailed speech on the cutthroat. Her comments were rich with information to the delight of the nerdiest of policy wonks and fish lovers. Many of the legislators, media, and assorted fish enthusiasts assembled to watch the press conference dozed off at times despite Grace's spellbinding fish tales.

Once Grace wrapped up her remarks, she took a few questions from reporters without a hitch. All appeared to be calm, and the conference appeared to be coming to a close, when out of nowhere, chaos splashed onto the scene. State Representative Alfred Gill, firebrand from Whitefish, popped out from behind a crowd of schoolchildren to ask a question.

"Grace, do you have a few minutes to answer some questions today?" Representative Gill said. "Something is fishy." Even the school kids were horrified by the fish pun, but they were about to see the destruction of the proposed legislation and the firm's spokesperson that resembled the gutting of a catfish.

Grace signaled with a nod that she had time and gestured to Gill, known best around the capital for his deep pockets used to grab snacks at the many free food receptions for legislators and his impressive suspenders collection, which supported his equally impressive and growing waistline.

"Your bill seeks to exonerate the spotted cutthroat trout for its crimes, is that correct?" said Gill.

"Well, no, sir, the spotted cutthroat trout isn't actually violent; it's just a name." Grace said.

"In fact, hasn't the cutthroat harmed a lot of other fish?"

"Uh, no, Representative Gill. The fish hasn't hurt anyone," Grace said.

"So you're saying if I were to say I had people willing to testify to the cutthroat nature of this fish, you would be calling me a liar?" Gill said. "I have underwater footage of this dangerous fish attacking the fish that inspired the naming of my fair city. I have sworn affidavits from twelve people who claim that the fish has, in fact, cut throats and has killed other fish."

The entire state of Montana, much of it assembled in the rotunda, collectively gasped. Within hours, I realized that, much like the fictional victims of the now-dreaded spotted cutthroat trout, the legislation was dead.

This hearing had veered off course in an unexpected way. Grace endured a series of obscure fish-related inquiries that left her looking like she herself had been attacked by an angry cutthroat. While Gill was well within his rights to ask these questions, I wondered how this man had gotten such detailed, inside, and explosive information about the spotted cutthroat trout. He didn't know a fish from a food truck! In fact, Gill had been, up until the press conference, a guy who had spent most of his legislative career focused solely on creating a museum for Evel Knievel, pride of Butte, Montana. He had narrowly lost a bid for a state license plate that would have said "Do Good by Supporting Evel."

While in Montana, I didn't know the answer for how he got the loaded information. That changed quickly upon getting back home.

Once back at the firm, I realized that the recording of the press conference had become must-see TV. It was analyzed in the firm's offices and break rooms every bit as much as the Zapruder tapes.

Rewind!

No, let's fast forward to when Grace's head spins around!

Aargh, now here comes the part where he throws a dead fish at Grace!

Part interrogation and part shaming, Grace received a legislative waterboarding for all the press corps and her colleagues at the firm to see.

I was wrapping up my work for the week and prepared to leave. Packing my bag of "homework" for the weekend, I began to walk out the door. As I left, I noticed Hazel was still in her office. I stopped and commented about how badly the hearing had gone and wondered about its impact on the firm, our client, and our colleague Grace.

Hazel and I did not talk much, other than a recap of what had occurred in the hearing and the potential risk and fallout merited our collaboration and discussion.

"Hazel, can you believe that happened? What a disaster!" I said.

"Grace deserved it. That went even better than planned!" crowed Hazel.

All I could hear was "planned."

"Planned? Did you say planned?" I asked.

She said, "I can't take full credit for the questions, but Al was on his game. Did you see "Graceless" up there? I thought she was going to cry. Serves her right. I hate the witch. Cecil could not stop laughing!"

"Can't take full credit?" Now my head was spinning.

The arsonist had just bragged and now seemed to be brimming with confidence.

I stewed on this horrifying admission over the weekend. Suzy made the most sense to discuss the facts with, but she had long since shown that she was worried only about herself. I even envisioned Suzy explaining this to be Hazel's triumphant effort to assist others in furthering democracy. This reached such a level of seriousness—and recklessness—that I felt obligated to talk directly with Cecil.

On Monday, I looked into Cecil's office, and he waved me in while he completed a call.

"Morning, Pete, have a good weekend?" he asked.

"It was great, but I really need to cut to the chase," I said, not disguising my emotions and purpose for being there. "It's about the cutthroat press conference and Grace."

He laughed, then got up and walked past me to close his door. "It was hilarious, wasn't it? Did you see Grace's face? She looked historical. Our fish friends in Montana didn't need that bill anyway. It was overkill. We'll survive, and they'll be fine."

"I don't disagree about overkill, but Hazel took credit for what happened to Grace in the hearing," I replied.

And I think you mean hysterical!

For the first and only time, the always verbally prolific Cecil froze. I don't know if he had any idea of what Hazel was referring to, and he was not going to respond directly to my news.

"Pete, stop. I don't even want to hear what you're getting at. I don't have long until I become an Emeritus Partner. I don't need this. We never talked; do you understand?" And with that, Cecil had just shut the door on hearing anymore about the hearing, but I naively thought that more explanation could change his understanding

"You can't be serious. Our client's project was just blown up. You're not concerned about that?" I sputtered.

"Two. More. Years. Left."

Looking the other way may not matter—until it is actually matters a great deal. The impact of not taking action on the deeds of an arsonist may never be necessary. On the other hand, you may be forced to deal with them in a deposition, a financial payout, the loss of a client, or a call from a reporter wondering who knew what and when?

When it comes to coddling the arsonists in the office, it's up to management to make the call.

Chapter Fifteen

FIREPROOFING
YOUR CAREER

Preston had left. Suzy had buckled. Brad had bolted. Jen got jolted. Alice had been axed. Grace had been gutted, and I was trying to simply survive another day in this place.

I was constantly trying to play a game of defense, and it was exhausting. What I needed to do was go on the offensive. Not as a jerk. Not as an arsonist. I needed to proactively and positively fight blow for blow when attacked. There is no more important thing you can do in your career than to take challenges to your work head-on and demonstrate your value and success.

What can you to do to combat the arsonist in your office—whether the arsonist is your coworker, your boss, or the whole corrupt culture?

You need to fireproof yourself. Here are twenty-one ways to keep you from being burned by an arsonist and also take you to the next level in any job in any organization:

1. Become an untouchable, too. Arsonists in the office are usually high performers. Work just as hard and become an untouchable because of your productivity.

2. Be visible. Volunteer on committees, charitable efforts, and anything else that will get notice—and, as a bonus, may get you out of the office for a mental health break.

3. Stay away from gossips. They will get you in trouble every time.

4. Build coalitions. As in politics, building alliances works. The more friends you have, the better chance you have to survive workplace warfare.

5. Know who your friends are—and *aren't*. Only discuss what you have to about yourself, and before you start talking about your life, your frustrations on the job, and anything else, ask the question "Can what I'm saying be twisted and used against me?" Here's how it could go: "I heard Employee X talking about a great weekend party and the great margaritas they served . . . think X is an alcoholic?" Be careful of what you say at work!

6. Let no attack go unanswered. If rumors being spread about you, fight back with the truth.

7. Document everything—*everything*! If you're asked to do something questionable, put your concern in writing. Do not just hope that you can defend yourself. Documentation is a way to watch your back.

8. Watch for strange changes in behaviors or communications. Is someone no longer speaking to you, who previously talked up a storm? Arsonists and those affected by arsonists betray their feelings in various ways. Hazel, much like a shark, would disappear from sight shortly before an attack. Watch for the changes.

9. Show no weakness. If the arsonist is coming after you, don't flinch. Respond and inform others.

10. Advertise your achievements. And remember that the best advertising doesn't *feel* like advertising. In other words, subtly show your value. Use victories in your job as a way to compliment everyone who helped you. When you do, you'll solidify your alliances even more.

11. Explain your value. Don't assume people know what you do. They probably don't. Ensuring that people understand you understand what you do and the value you bring to the company is not only important in toxic environments but also in every situation.

12. Always be ethical. Nervous about being muscled out of a company? Be smart by not being stupid. Don't pad your expense reports, don't do anything in front of or with your coworkers that you don't want blamed exclusively on you, and don't sign off on anything you are uncomfortable with. If someone wants to try and get you removed from your position—be it as a CEO or as a paper clip counter—your adversaries will look for dirt. Don't give them any places to look.

13. Do favors across departmental lines. Get to know people in other segments of your organization. If you face challenges, it's best to have friends in as many parts of the organization as possible.

14. Become as versatile as possible. Know your job, and learn how to do other tasks within the company.

15. Make yourself indispensable. Find that one thing you can call your own that no one else knows how to do or knows how to do well. For instance, it's no secret that many businesses utilize Microsoft Excel as a tool. However, my experi-

ence is that very few people know how to use it well. Find out what that thing is and make it your own.

16. Be a team player. No matter how productive you might be individually, people remember if you helped them.

17. Be a note taker. Taking notes will put you ahead of virtually everyone else who attends most business meetings. That's a plus because people will rely on your recollections in meetings. Taking notes of what is happening in a toxic workplace can also be helpful as they are a potential tool you can use to defend yourself against accusations and bad behavior. Contemporaneous notes, as they're called, assist in fighting what's known as "memory decay" and may pay dividends at some point if you are being attacked by a coworker and need to document your experiences. Our memories are easily changed by passage of time, the recollections of others, later life events, stress, and other motives. Former FBI Director James Comey has made contemporaneous notes famous by detailing his recollections of conversations he said he had with President Donald Trump.

Contemporaneous notes are used as evidence in courtrooms, if for no other reason than they carry more weight than mere recollections that you pull from the tip of your tongue. Not necessarily from a legal standpoint, but from the perspective of your company's executives, it is very possible that they do not want to see these notes become public and, as a result, these notes could protect you if things get ugly. And these notes can come in handy for executives, too. If you are dealing with unscrupulous people, no matter what level of the food chain they're on, use the tools you have to explain your side of the story. Cases are decided upon evidence, and documentation is critical. When taking notes, use email or software that provides a timestamp for when the document was written.

18. "Is this thing on?" Don't do this!

In talking to people in researching the topic of protecting yourself in the workplace, several of them brought up the concept of recordings—either audio or video—to protect themselves in toxic situations. It's definitely easy to do, as anyone with a smartphone has a recording device in their pocket. Lots of states allow one-person consent for an audio recording—thirty-eight in total. However, there are numerous states that allow companies to prohibit recording from taking place in a workplace. But here's the bottom-line thing to know. No matter the kind words you might get from investigative teams in the media, and no matter how many strangers will think you're cool because of your courage, know that you can doom your career immeasurably and permanently if you record someone. Don't do it. You can't cash in a high-five from another disgruntled coworker and pay your mortgage with it.

Don't do it.

Abar Rouse can tell you something about what happens to people that secretly record others. Rouse was an up-and-coming assistant basketball coach at Baylor University under former Coach Dave Bliss for a brief stint in 2003. His time at Baylor came during a scandal involving the murder of basketball player Patrick Dennehy by a former teammate, allegations of payments to athletes, Bliss paying for the tuition of Dennehy, rumors of rampant drug use, and the subsequent attempt to cover up all matters involved.

In an effort to whitewash the facts and throw investigators off the trail, Bliss told his players and his assistant coaches to tell investigators Dennehy had paid for his tuition through drug deals. This storyline was intended to protect Bliss from blowback for paying for Dennehy's tuition. Rouse, in an effort to protect himself and to protect Dennehy's name from being sullied unnecessarily, recorded the conversation. While Rouse says he did not make the recording public, the tape ended up in the hands of the media. Rouse, while hailed publicly as a hero, has been blackballed by the coaching profession.

In response to a question about an assistant recording, legendary Duke basketball coach Mike Krzyzewski told ESPN's *Outside the Lines* in 2003, "If one of my assistants would tape every one of my conversations with me not knowing it, there's no way he would be on my staff."[1] Syracuse head coach Jim Boeheim echoed Krzyzewski's comments in a different interview.

Not only did Rouse not remain at Baylor, but he was blackballed from coaching in basketball after the recording incident. He now teaches GED preparation to federal prisoners in Fort Worth, Texas. Rouse told journalist Mike Wise in an interview for The Undefeated, an ESPN website, that he believes he did the right thing but knows it came at a price.

"At some point in everybody's career, you're going to have to face an ethical question. For me, I drew the line at a dead body," said Rouse.[2] And his career.

19. Follow the "*Washington Post* Rule." It's 2018. Nothing is private. One of my favorite supervisors had a great policy for written communications: "If you do not want to see your email on the front page of the *Washington Post,* don't send it." That made our decisions easy. Put nothing in an email that you would not be comfortable having read by your supervisor or your CEO. Your company emails are not private and can be used against you. Understand that your communications can be monitored—in healthy companies or toxic ones. The *Washington Post* rule will always keep you safe from an unforced error.

20. Guard your other personal communications. *Wait a second, I am chatting on Facebook Messenger! My company can't read those!*, you might think. And, if you thought this, you're wrong if you're using a company device. If you are using a company phone, your organization may be be able to capture your information. Depending on the software installed on your work phone, the information in your emails through Yahoo, Google, or other personal email accounts, as well as internet searches, can be captured through keystroke logger software. If you are mixing personal texts and work texts together on your work phone, your company can see both, even if they are not doing it intentionally. If there is a legal matter, they can also request personal account emails that mention work in some way. I repeat: write nothing you do not want your employers to read. When you leave a company, delete the information that would allow access to personal email accounts. The easiest way to keep electronic messages private is to buy a separate phone for personal use, assume everything you write in an email can be used against you in the future, and don't write anything you don't want your company to read.

21. Beware of reviews and surveys in toxic environments. A "360 review" is a process that allows an employee to be reviewed from a variety of directions—from a supervisor, a coworker, and even subordinates. Much like emails, know that few things are anonymous, and you can be harmed greatly by your responses.

Dan, a mid-level manufacturing executive in the Southeast US, had been concerned for years about his supervisor's unwanted and aggressive flirting with him and his coworkers. He saw the 360 review as a great way to pass along information with a level of discretion and without confrontation. He felt surprised but empowered when it was announced that his supervisor had been terminated and word spread within his division that she had been fired because of allegations of sexual harassment and a brief investigation.

But his victory was short-lived, as he was terminated just days later. The company may have needed to deal with Dan's boss because of written comments they felt compelled to investigate. However, Dan learned later that his allegation, though backed up by others, forced management to take an action that they felt pressured to take. As a result, Dan wins. But then loses big. It's just one more reason to know exactly how your company deals with conflict. And how it deals with people who point out problems no matter how benignly. On this issue, I highly recommend perusing Chapter 19.

Regarding surveys, if you have concerns about anonymity, do not fill out the survey if you have concerns about the questions. It's all about trust because a lot of anonymous surveys are not as anonymous as you might think. The questions about job satisfaction, your views on your manager, and many other questions can profile you as disgruntled depending on the mindset of the person reading the questions. In most companies, they are looking for input to help the company get stronger. In a toxic workplace, they may be looking for something else entirely.

The bottom line? Implement these twenty-one tactics in all that you do and you'll be better protected, more plugged in, and in a stronger position to succeed in all that you do. Now, the question is, if your workplace is as bad as the one I encountered at the firm, do you want to stay or go?

Chapter Sixteen

FIRE DRILLS

I hate fire drills, but they're important. They train you how to safely evacuate in a stressful, dangerous time. When working with an arsonist or in a toxic workplace, you might reach that day that feels like the point of no return. Especially when dealing with a toxic workplace, you need to proactively think through how you're going to exit.

If you're in a toxic workplace, you may think every day about quitting. But your plan needs to be to leave on your own with a job in hand. Don't quit except for one of two reasons: health or if you already have another job waiting for you. If a job is wrecking your physical health or breaking you psychologically, I can't blame you if you need to leave a job immediately. Go. I can't fault you for doing it, but read on about what you'll face on the other side and see if it's still worth it.

Otherwise, plan to do one of a couple of things: think through whether you can switch departments within your company if your problem is within your department, or methodically plan your exit.

Regarding staying at your company, is your problem isolated within a department or is the entire company the problem? There's a big difference between the two. Talk to people who have transferred from one department to another if you haven't done it before and find out how it works. They may be able to coach you through the dos and don'ts. Of course, if you can no longer handle working for your company, it's time to devise your exit strategy.

If you think you need to leave, there are some big things to think about that can and should affect your timeline. Ask yourself these questions:

- Is your resume up to date?

- Do you have a LinkedIn profile?

- Do you have a recent headshot for pictures?

- When was the last time you sat through an interview?

- Do you have an online brand? If so, think about what it is. If it's not professional, clean it up. Enter your name into a search engine and see what shows up on the first few pages. If you tend to pop off with hot opinions on Twitter and Facebook, make the delete button your friend. If you don't have any brand at all, start with LinkedIn and go from there.

- Can you secure a reference from a trustworthy person at your current employer?

- Have you talked with all of your job references in the last two years? If not, talk to them. It's a good opportunity to reconnect; it's also a good way to find out if everyone on your list of references is still a friend! There are companies you can find online that will call your references and pose as an organization calling about a job. If you have concerns about what any of your references might say, connect with one of those companies.

- Are you networking? If not, start now. According to a February 2016 survey by Lou Adler, CEO of The Adler Group, 85 percent of respondents said that they found their job through networking.[1] That's pretty powerful.

- What skills do you need to not only move out but also to move up? Find out. And if you have a weakness, address it.

Meanwhile, if you're one of the people reading this book thinking you can't take your toxic company for another minute, simply don't quit your job unless you have something else ready. Don't step up to the line of quitting. Don't have any conversations that make people think you're planning to leave.

Never give anyone any idea that could leave you in the job market without a job.

You'll read more about my exit from the firm, but let me tell you this—there's one thing worse than being disrespected, disenchanted, hated, sabotaged, played for a fool, gaslighted, intimidated, demoralized and otherwise ticked off at work: it's looking for a job while not employed.

It's brutal.

Here are some things to consider:

- Financially, do you have cash that can get you through the time it will take you to find a job? One traditional rule of thumb has been that for every $10,000 of salary, it will take you a month to find a job. So, for a $100,000 salary, plan as if you'll be on the shelf for ten months or more.

- How specialized is your career—are you in a niche field?

If so, you have no idea how hard it will be to find a job without a job when you are competing against employed applicants. Know the answer to this question.

- Be aware of the new scarlet letter: It's "U." Companies may not tell you, but many have a policy—written or unwritten—that they don't hire unemployed people. It's not as easy to sell an unemployed person's attributes. Prepare mentally to lose out in job searches regularly.

- Sharpen your narrative. When you start to interview, you will likely be asked why you left your job. If you can't do it without bashing your previous employer or don't have a plausible response without mentioning numerous red flags, you have a problem. Your narrative needs to be positive even though you left under tough circumstances.

- References—or a lack thereof. It's tough to secure a reference from your toxic employer if your last discussion with your employer was made up mostly of four-letter words. If you quit, know that you will be asked why you left your last job.

- Limited choice of jobs. You'll lose out on top-tier jobs because you aren't working currently. That leaves you a rummage bin of options you may be shocked you're having to pick through. And you'll be forced to look at jobs well below your qualifications and your salary range.

- Your tolerance for suffering. Stress? Expect it. Self-doubt? It's a given. Feeling disconnected to friends? Mark my words.

Did I scare you enough? Good. Only leave your job with a job in hand. Plan your exit. Don't just run for the doors.

Chapter Seventeen

TORCHED

Some say that the definition of insanity is doing the same thing over and over again and expecting different results. It's not much different than Charlie Brown trusting Lucy to not pull away the football despite her doing it every time. Despite everything I was watching from Suzy and Cecil, I still held out hope that Hazel's actions would eventually catch up with her. Suzy and Cecil, after all, were smart people.

How did my speculation go? Let's just say Charlie Brown and I were apparently a lot alike in our optimism.

I couldn't un-see everything I had seen, especially watching how Alice had been fired. Nor the stalking. Or the bizarre lunch buffet. Or the sabotage. Or the attacks on other employees. Or on clients. Or . . . or . . . or. The list went on and on.

Knowing that changes needed to be made was obvious. Finding someone with any authority to acknowledge the obvious was another issue entirely.

The interests of clients were being threatened; staff was

being bullied, harassed, and targeted for termination; and the reputation of the firm was clearly at stake. What if members of Congress, state legislators, or our clients got a whiff of what was happening here?! I wanted to talk to Cecil, as he knew better than anyone the stakes involved.

I asked him for an opportunity to meet, and he said to show up at his office bright and early the next morning.

I got to the office early and was ready for action. In our meeting I presented a series of tangible moves that would make the firm stronger, solve problems, and lessen the drama. Of course, the plan would have given me some breathing room, too, affording me clearly divided lines of responsibility and clarified titles to avoid at least some of the mischief I faced during the last several congressional sessions and for the organization to deal with some of Hazel's more peculiar behaviors. I talked about all the sabotaged work, harassment of coworkers and outsiders, the constant threats, the rogue lobbying efforts, the lunch from hell, the cross-country meeting stalking, and the cutthroat con artistry.

His comments that followed were a perfect medley of stunned and sedate as he ran through the rap sheet I detailed.

"I wondered why you were all 'deer in the headlights' sometimes in your presentations.

"She did that at lunch? You eaten Chinese food since, son?"

"You told anybody she's showing up at your meetings? Nobody can hear about that. Oh Lordy! Ha, ha!"

"Havel, you could write a book!" (I think this serves as tacit encouragement to your humble author.)

Cecil, always affable, with an ear especially attuned for anything that could detract from his successful track record, apologized. As hollow as it was, it felt good in some way to hear something that acknowledged this madhouse.

"I really am not surprised, and I'm sorry. I'd throw a net over some of this place if I were you," he said. Then he added, "Pete, I'm surprised you have wanted to stay around as long as you have. I think I told you that when you got here. Congratulations for putting up with it. You ought to be proud!"

I really should have pushed for the employee of the month award after the lunch, I thought.

While I appreciated him understanding the challenges, he seemed more entertained than awakened.

Once done with the kudos, Cecil pivoted to a series of questions. This should have given me a glimpse into exactly where this was headed. Familiar questions about who knew what, if I knew when his retirement would kick in, and why he was ducking Hazel in every way he could.

I was disgusted, but I couldn't show it. He was my only chance to make my life any better or this job tolerable.

"I want you to stay, Pete. You'll be here as long as you want to be here, and I'll see what I can do. Send me a plan," he said.

I thought I had just presented him a plan, but I thought he possibly wanted it in another form. I gave him the plan the next day—exactly what he and I had just discussed but arranged a little differently. Cecil said he would think about what he could do.

Days turned into weeks. I was getting impatient, as this was dragging on much longer than it needed to.

When I had been waiting nearly a month, I asked for a meeting with Cecil and Suzy to talk about my plan and next steps. To my surprise, they agreed quickly. We went from "hurry up and wait" to "go time" and set plans to meet the next afternoon. I was realistic but encouraged.

Why wouldn't they want to make changes? I thought.

The next day, the three of us met. We sat down at a small table in the corner of the room. Suzy started to speak, but Cecil raced to shut the door before any discussion began.

"Suzy, let me start, and you can chime in," Cecil said.

"Sure, Cecil," she replied.

Cecil began the meeting with more of the same: secrecy, apologies, a joint discussion of their retirement plan trajectory, an interrogation over who knew what, agreement on the overall awkwardness of the situation, and another demand for secrecy.

Among all of that, I squeezed in a few words about the plan I had submitted.

"This plan looks good, but not a word, Pete," Cecil instructed.

"I won't say a thing, Cecil. I just want some help."

I was skeptical of major changes, but I had trust in the firm to allow me to leave on my own terms if I wanted to or stay if I wanted to put up with this foolishness in the future. Cecil himself had promised me that.

After the meeting, I went home and talked with my wife about everything that had been happening.

I had kept most things bottled up, preferring not to talk about the drama inside the office. If you have read much of anything in this book, can you imagine bringing home these stories for dinnertime discussion?

"How was your day, dear?"

"Before or after I got flashed at lunch?"

Or "Tell me about your job, Dad."

"Well, sweetheart, do you want the G version or the PG-13?"

It was strange enough for me to deal with every day, much less forcing my family to deal with this occupational clown car.

As I laid out some of the many challenges and incidents I had been facing, my wife told me about an incident of her own in very recent times—a detailed story about a large luncheon that had taken place with a not-so-welcome visitor.

What happened became a turning point.

As part of her job as a bank president in our community, my wife gets recognized at local events like Rotary and Kiwanis Club events. The day of that lunch was no exception as she stood and was thanked by the local organization for her bank's sponsorship. Moments later, while a hushed crowd of 400 people listened to the featured speaker deliver his talk, a bobbing and weaving, high-heel-wearing diva of discord fishtailed through the sea of tables and headed straight for my wife. As she approached, she slid in beside my wife, kneeled next to her, and began whispering into her ear a series of verbal assaults on me that were intended to strike a match and throw it into the gasoline tank.

I won't tell you who it was, but I'll spot you an H, an A, and a Z to get you started.

Amazingly, after Hazel was done with the trash talking, she handed my wife a business card, smiled sweetly to the table, and marched out of the room, waving to any who gazed upon her.

Hazel had been coming after me through any avenue possible—but now we had entered a whole new dimension of impropriety—she was gaslighting my wife.

A line had been crossed.

I didn't know if my next action should involve the firm or law enforcement.

This was not a chance interaction, a bumping into someone in a crowded room. She had navigated an obstacle course of hundreds of people to plop herself down and drag my spouse into her dysfunction. I had no earthly idea of what to expect next.

* * *

Water heaters have pressure release valves. They're used to reduce overheating and alleviate pressure. If the valve isn't operating correctly, water heaters can turn into bombs. Cars have speed governors to ensure stability and safety. Most of us have a governor of sorts on our internal engines—it's called our conscience. It's often exhibited through our personal moral codes or our faith. Hazel's actions made me question whether her governor was operational. I didn't think I could be surprised by anything Hazel did anymore, but this action left me speechless.

Her move was surely calculated to get a response. It got one.

The next morning, I immediately asked Suzy if we could meet. She waved me into her office, and I laid out exactly what had occurred. I wanted to know from her own mouth how this breach of every piece of workplace decorum imaginable was going to be addressed. My tone was powerful but respectful. However, I was not going to leave this alone.

You may be wondering why I would go to Suzy with such a matter after having talked to Cecil previously. The reason is that, frankly, I thought this was so easy of a discussion to have that even Suzy would understand the need for action.

"Suzy, you are now aware that Hazel confronted my wife. What you are going to do to make sure this never happens again?" I said.

"Pete, this may have been Hazel wanting to promote good customer service. I'm sure you misunderstood. Hazel is very outgoing."

"And Jeffrey Dahmer was just hungry. Are you kidding? Please tell me you're kidding." No, she wasn't kidding.

We had suddenly gone from Stockholm syndrome to Baghdad Bob. While American tanks were literally rolling through the streets of Baghdad in 2003, Saddam Hussein's spokesman Muhammad Saeed al-Sahhaf (a.k.a., "Baghdad Bob") proclaimed, "There are no American infidels in Baghdad. Never!"[1]

The idea that Hazel confronting my wife was a business activity was surreal.

I was led through Suzy's usual topics that preceded any conversation of great import: retirement, etc., etc.

I was seething, and I'm sure my body language betrayed my disgust. Suzy wrapped up the meeting mumbling about calls she had to make.

I continued to press her.

"Suzy, will you be saying anything to Hazel about this?"

"I'm not going to discuss what I may do," she said.

And, looking back, she was right. She didn't. She never spoke to me. And from that point on, everything changed.

Over the next two weeks, as I prepared for a major "Year in Review" briefing about the success my team and I had enjoyed in the last congressional term, the remarkably social Suzy became silent.

Do you remember the game Wonderball? In elementary school, my classmates and I sat in a circle and passed the ball around until the Wonderball song stopped. When the song ended, whoever was left holding the ball was out of the game.

Hazel was Suzy's wonderball, and she did not want to get stuck holding this rolling ball of knives. Not as long as the retirement package was still just a matter of a few short terms away. Cecil had thrown Hazel in Suzy's lap. If this incident escalated as I expect they thought it would, Cecil would have thrown Suzy under the bus. Suzy had to figure out how to contain this fire. I wasn't looking for a managerial miracle, but an apology, common sense changes, and a promise that this bizarre act would never be tolerated by the organization would have certainly been appreciated.

Suzy had no idea of how this situation would end. If word got out, Cecil would throw her under the bus, and her Emeritus Partner retirement package would become a pipe dream. The storyline was explosive. If you're the firm—and in particular, Suzy or Cecil—how do you explain the breadth of Suzy's actions to your leadership, the media, in a court proceeding or to law enforcement? While not mentioning nor contemplating contacting any of those entities, I am confident that minds were racing.

To quiet any potential problems, it was Suzy's turn to become the arsonist. Remember, one of the things an arsonist does is burn things down to distract from or eliminate other problems.

After my meeting with Suzy, something felt wrong, but I didn't know what. Suzy was not responding to most of my emails, but I held out hope that she was just giving me space. But in other ways, this felt different.

While on a business trip to meet with clients in Chicago, a strange meeting invitation email popped up in my inbox.

It was a message from Suzy asking me to attend a "planning meeting" with just the two of us in a room so obscure that I didn't even know it existed. It felt strangely familiar—like something out of a movie.

You know, the movies where a character gets a mysterious phone call asking to meet in a mysterious dark warehouse near the docks. That person always ends up kidnapped, assaulted, or dead.

I had a feeling that my job was about to face a similar fate.

After Suzy's email, I got an unusual call from a member of the firm's Board of Overseers, Bart. He was on a fishing expedition.

"Pete, I'm hearing rumors about you. What can you tell me?" he began.

"The reports of my death are an exaggeration," I volleyed, delivering Mark Twain's famous quote as well as I could.

"Well, I just wondered how you were," he said, prodding further. It was the conversational equivalent of putting a mirror over someone's mouth to detect life.

"You're asking about my job, right?" I asked.

"Well, yeah," he meandered. "I am hearing things."

"Let me just boil it down. I have been working with Hazel for—" I said.

But before I could even complete the thought, he said, "I've got a few stories to tell you. Do you have a minute?" He should have asked me if I had thirty minutes, as he spent the next half hour sharing his own stories, both what he had heard about Hazel and experienced himself. It was a greatest hits album of Hazel's antics.

"You know all of this, and you're on the board, Bart. You know exactly what I'm facing. Will you help me?"

Upon that request, Bart began verbally tap-dancing like he was Fred Astaire. "I've had to deal with this person before, and I know what they're capable of," he volunteered, shaken so much he would not mention Hazel's name despite continuing to allude to her for the next ten minutes. "I wish you well, and let me know if I can ever be of help. I'll be happy to be a reference. Good luck."

Click.

Bart's call represented the full corruption of a culture. In organizations you have many levels of people with responsibilities: the rank-and-file employees, the executive leadership, and those with fiduciary roles like members of boards of overseers. The board is supposed to be the backbone of the organization—those who guide the ship when no one else can or the ones who are charged with bringing an organization back to its true north when things go south. But when fiduciaries are abdicating their responsibilities? Game. Set. Match. The culture is cooked.

As he ended the call, my flight began to board. The flight allowed me valuable time to think through my game plan—or, to be honest, *think* of a game plan. While little was under my control in this process, I was adamant that I would maintain my dignity and not be part of any process that involved the absurd perp-walk-style process the firm was reportedly famous for—where an employee is marched out of the office.

When I landed, I headed straight to the office to pack up. I collected my things, loaded up my truck, and spent the next couple of hours driving around. I hadn't told my wife just yet, as I wanted to be 100 percent certain I was right about what was happening. I would have felt like a real jerk if it all turned out to be a false alarm.

I didn't sleep that night, as I tossed and turned throughout a fitful few hours of rest. All I could think about was the meeting to come. I asked the good Lord for strength, wisdom, and the capacity to not say anything I would ultimately regret.

When I woke up early the next morning, scattered and conflicting thoughts went through my mind. Fear and relief. Desperation and hope.

For some unexplainable reason, I was feeling good—exceptionally good. Prayer does that. I got in my car and arrived promptly for the most awkward and unintentionally amusing firing in modern history.

When I got to the office, I practically needed a tour guide and a passport to find the secret location. After a room search that would have made Vasco da Gama proud, I entered, just a few minutes before our 9:00 a.m. kickoff. Suzy came in a minute later, followed shortly by HR Harry, who was not on the guest list.

Eye contact was nonexistent, as neither could take their eyes off of the papers they brought into the meeting.

Harry brought the meeting to order. "Well, Pistol Pete, I guess you know what this meeting is all about."

"Is this where we discuss Hazel confronting my wife?" I replied, expecting the comment to immediately disappear from his consciousness.

"Uh, we are relieving you of your position," he said.

"And on what grounds?" I asked, twisting the knife just a bit.

"I would rather not get into it," said Harry.

The "it," of course, was going to be tricky for even Harry to explain.

Across the table from me, Suzy had crossed into another dimension. While Harry prattled on about the seriousness of the matter and pontificated as though he was about to offer a toast with all the lofty rhetoric he was emitting, Suzy was in distress. Instead of crouching into the fetal position, she was drawing pictures furiously. A flower. A dog. A sunset. Then she repeatedly wrote her name in a bubbly script, as though she were practicing it. For what it's worth, her penmanship was beautiful.

I continued to look at Harry as he finished his eulogy. After five minutes or so, I couldn't wait any longer. I had to ask a question that at that point was the 800-pound gorilla in the room.

"Suzy, are you really drawing during this meeting?!"

At that point, she began to either cry or perspire. I could relate—a few more minutes of this, and I'd be sweating, too.

Harry looked over, grabbed a peek at her sketches, and correctly surmised that he was losing his grip on this meeting.

With a best practices must-say of "Well, I don't know what to tell ya," he shoved a folder across the table with some papers that included a few dollar signs.

"Decide what you want to do. You only have a few days."

Not having read the paperwork, I gave him the most affirmative comment I could muster. "I'll read it over and let you know."

I handed over my security badge to Harry. He informed me that my belongings in my office would be delivered to my home.

I said, "No need to do that. I packed everything up last night," thinking I had just saved them time and effort.

This began a series of looks and under-the-breath comments back and forth between the duo as they began whispering about whether the other had told me what was going to happen to me prior to this meeting. With mouths not moving but words coming out, they had morphed into a pair of frustrated ventriloquists. They were fighting about who they thought spilled the beans!

"I didn't tell him."

"Who told him?"

"Did you tell him?"

"I can hear you two. It's OK. You can surprise me next time," I said.

If I had known the meeting to terminate me was going to

be this bad, I would have fired myself!

We all rose to our feet without prompting, signaling the end of the get-together. I grabbed keys and my prize package from HR.

Suzy fled in one direction while Harry walked me out in the other. With his hand on my elbow, he gestured toward the door, and we walked outside toward a courtyard area. As we got outside of anyone's earshot, he looked around and then popped off one last time.

With a threat.

"You need to sign that document, Pistol Pete."

"OK, I'll read it over," I said, legitimately confused about where this conversation was going.

"You don't want to fight me on this."

I looked down at the document trying to figure out where this conversation was going. I felt him invading my personal space.

But as I looked up, I realized he was not leaning into me to intimidate, but to get something out of his pocket. He and his pants were wrestling over whatever was in there, and he was leaning over to get it out. Finally, the tug of war between Harry and his pants ended. He was a triumphant winner. He began to unfold and iron out a now-crumped and slightly ripped piece of paper. It had the feel of a note I might have passed in high school. Was I about to be invited to a prom?

After reaching his optimum level of un-creasing, he presented the masterpiece.

I did a quick scan of the now-unfolded paper and looked at him with a mix of pity and disbelief.

"You've got to be kidding me," I muttered.

It was a printout showing how much the organization had paid lawyers the year before.

"You punch me, I'll punch back, Pistol Pete. This could get expensive for you if you want to fight."

Harry's delivery was a mix of mall cop and game show host. *"OK, Pistol Pete, you can take a small amount of financial security and walk away today with the prize package. Or you can risk it all, not take the severance benefits, and I'll bury you with legal fees behind door number three,"* I imagined him saying.

"Are we clear?"[2] he said, suddenly channeling his inner Col. Jessup from *A Few Good Men.*

Strangely amused at a not-so-funny time, I responded with the only appropriate response I could muster: "Crystal,"[3] I said.

My last minutes at the firm had descended into a community theater audition, mixed with the bizarre threat of a legal fight. And always with the "Pistol Pete" that not another living soul has ever called me.

As with all theater, however, there is always a final act. For this, Cecil stepped onto the stage. Just days after my termination, he reached out and proclaimed that he would be happy to serve as a reference for me. I assume that his call was an act of remorse, but his call is both a reason for hope and also a warning to anyone who finds themselves in a toxic organization.

As for the hope, Cecil still had an operational soul and understood what he had done to my family and me. He said it outright. And he probably knew exactly how he was serving in his capacity at the firm. This was his act of assistance, as filled with contradiction and as vapid as it was.

As for the warning, the remorse did nothing to change his actions. His inability to lead boldly and address his widely acknowledged problem inadvertently served as the death knell for my time there. A kindly leader inside a corrupted organization will not err on the side of the right thing if it causes inconvenience.

While Cecil obviously felt regret, at the end of the day, his self-preservation and glorious retirement plan mattered far more.

And from there, as you'll soon hear, it was time to rebuild.

But first, a thought haunted me. *Could I have avoided all of this?*

And, in the future, can you? I'm going to show you how to reduce the odds of ever ending up in an organization like the firm.

Chapter Eighteen

FIREWATCHING—TIPS, TOOLS, AND TACTICS FOR AVOIDING THE TOXIC WORKPLACE

The thought lingered with me for a long time: Was there something I could have done to have caught a whiff of the craziness of the firm and avoid the situation completely?

Until I joined the firm, I never thought about doing in-depth research on employers. I thought I could handle anything. I was bulletproof.

I didn't how wrong I was until I was in the middle of toxic hell.

The sad thing was, I knew what to do to prevent joining a toxic company all along. It's what I did for work for a long time: opposition research.

When I researched those with opposing viewpoints, I

would find out everything I possibly could about where they went to school, how many kids they had, what their political leanings were, how long they'd been at their company, their likes, their dislikes—you name it.

When I worked on political campaigns, I dug up things as obscure as a fifty-something's doctoral thesis written back in his twenties.

But why hadn't I put the same time and passion into researching the place that could make or break my future?

There's no reason to guess or wonder about what a company is like when you can find out much of what you need to know. Information is out there, whether on the internet, within easy reach, or by using simple skills you already have. The information I'll share is also useful for companies trying to protect their reputations.

If you want to avoid working for a toxic company or reduce the need for a reboot of your company's reputation, become a firewatcher.

FIREWATCHING

During the height of World War II, as Nazi planes dropped bombs out of the skies over Great Britain, citizens began actively watching for explosion-generated fires. This was the birth of firewatching, an early warning system that allowed the British to plan for rescues and cleanup, perform damage assessments, and of course, put out fires.

Businesses and prospective job candidates need to engage in firewatching, too. Bombs may not literally be dropping, but there is always the potential for fires that could consume your organization before you know what hits you. Find out what you need to know before you're locked into a job, not after.

With these ten firewatching tactics and tools in your job search, you'll have what you need to research the culture and avoid the arsonists. Plus, you'll improve your interviewing skills dramatically.

1. Review the reviews. As an author, I am very interested in the reviews of this book on Amazon, Walmart, Apple, Goodreads, and so forth. The opinions on those sites shape people's views on a book. The same applies for company reviews by current and former employees on sites like Glassdoor and Indeed.

Glassdoor lets former and current employees rate a company's culture and values, pay, benefits, and even the CEO. Employees write in their own words about the company—which is where you will find the best information. As a benchmark, the average company rating is 3.4 (out of 5) and the average CEO rating is 69 percent. Ratings won't give you everything you need, but combine them with the comments, and it will start to paint a picture.

Indeed provides the same. Use them both, as not every employee is going to post on both sites.

Obviously, you'll see some bitter rants and some reviews that look to be pulled from company talking points. Ignore all of those. Look instead for patterns in the comments—good or bad.

2. Google them. Do the most obvious, but often most forgotten thing you can do to find out about a company: Google them! Enter the company's name into Google, Yahoo, or Bing, and see what pops up. From a toxicity standpoint, plug in words such as *lawsuit, harassment,* and *culture* along with the company name. Don't stop after the first page or two of search results, as they will not tell the full story. Savvy companies

know how to push bad news off the first few pages of search results, so keep digging until you feel satisfied.

3. Ignore shiny objects. In tight job markets, companies are working hard to bring in employees quickly to replace those who have left. The hiring process can feel like a used car lot sales pitch, so don't be swayed by the zero-to-sixty speeds and the smell of the leather seats because you may miss the crack in the engine block in the process. Ping pong tables, espresso machines, and goat yoga classes pale in comparison to good pay, a feeling of purpose, a solid culture, respect for your hard work, and management you can trust. Stay focused on the big stuff.

4. People watch. Watch everything. Of course, listen to what the person interviewing you is saying but use your time to watch the inner workings of the office. Do the employees look engaged or look like they're auditioning for *The Walking Dead*? Your interview is like a first date—the "getting to know you" phase. If there's no chemistry—or worse, a bad feeling in your gut—stay away.

5. Use your social media network. Do you have a profile on LinkedIn? If not, get one—it's one of the best ways to make connections between your friends and potential new contacts at companies. If you want to talk with former employees of the company where you have applied, use LinkedIn to find them and ask discretely if you can talk with them.

6. Evaluate the hiring process. The hiring process can tell you a lot about a company's culture. An efficient pace is good, but a process that feels too fast might mean the company is just trying to find a warm body—or you aren't getting the whole story as to why they're in such a rush. If a process drags on, it can mean a culture filled with procrastination or incom-

petence. Also, watch out if your interviewers are late or seem to be reading your resume for the first time when they're in front of you. If you think their lack of preparation is irritating now, just wait until you need to rely on them!

7. Interview the interviewers. Don't waste your time on softball questions or ask questions only to check the "Do you have any questions?' box. Good questions that will help you learn more about the company and the job include (1) "What are the most important qualities that someone needs in order to excel in this role?" (2) "Does the job provide growth opportunities?" and (3) "What are your expectations for this job in the first thirty, sixty, and ninety days?" On culture, ask your interviewers why they enjoy working there, and listen to their responses closely. Then ask them to tell you about the company's values and the culture. If they don't have much of an answer, you may have just learned a great deal.

8. Ask about turnover rates. The average turnover rate at US companies is between 11 and 12 percent. Some industries have lower rates and others much higher. Ask your interviewers how long they have worked for the company and the length of time people in the department you're interested in have worked for the company. Ask about the history of the position you are interviewing for. Have other people been in this role, or is it newly created? If it's an existing job, ask why the last person left, what they're doing now, and what challenges they faced that will be helpful for you to know.

9. Write down questions and look for patterns. Take notes in interviews. Doing these things not only makes you look more attentive and in command but also gives you better recall of everything that occurred when you unpack the interview's events later. Write down the questions you are asked.

Throughout the process, look for patterns in the questions. Years ago, I had an interview where half of the questions were about dealing with difficult people. Without notes, I wouldn't have noticed the pattern. I dropped out of the process soon after the interview and later learned I had dodged a bullet. The organization was a personnel train wreck.

10. Create your advisory team. Who do you know that can ask you hard questions and make you think? Make them part of your decision-making process. If you and a company are in serious discussions, you may have a decision to make. Do you want to work there? Is the company right for you? Be professional about it and, much like you would with other major decisions like investing, home purchases, and so forth, seek trusted advice. Run the opportunity by your smartest friends because you may not see things that they do, or your need for a new role may be overriding flashing warning signs that you are choosing not to see. What you decide to do and not do may shape or reshape your future. Be smart.

Now, onto business owners and managers.

Employee review sites like Glassdoor and Indeed should be very important to you. They're talking about you! My anecdotal research shows most executives are either not paying attention to these sites or passing the monitoring off to their HR team. That lax approach astounds me. Employees may be discussing civil rights violations, safety issues, lawsuits ready to happen, personal dalliances, or actually grading management performance—and they are ignoring the info or passing the buck. These sites can be your early warning system for major problems. Ignoring what is being said is done at your own peril.

Chapter Nineteen

SMOKE DETECTORS AND WHISTLEBLOWERS

Was I a whistleblower within the firm? Absolutely not.

Was I treated like one? Yep. When things get bad within a toxic organization, good employees can become the biggest threats.

Whether you have a concern about the arsonist in the office, the financing practice that doesn't seem legit, or you just tripped over someone's dirty little secret, you need to understand you may become a target if you mention the matter in even an informative or supportive way. Remember, in a war zone, collateral damage happens.

I'm not talking about leaking to the media, recording conversations, or other aggressive, outward-facing actions that would make any organization more than a bit concerned. I'm talking about warning someone in responsibility about a problem and becoming targeted for dismissal.

Secrecy is common in toxic workplaces, and cover-ups can be just as common. Often, the covering up involves your job being covered up—by dirt, in a shallow grave.

I call these people "smoke detectors" rather than whistleblowers because the concerns they raise may or may not have anything to do with broken laws. They're not attacking or undermining their employer. Rather, they're acting in the spirit of "see something, say something." But just as whistleblowers face blowback in some companies, smoke detectors can be targeted, too. They're regularly eliminated in toxic organizations and may never know what hit them.

ROSS

Ross was a procurement executive for a small government agency on the East Coast.

One morning, Ross got a call from a company that had won huge contracts with his agency. In a stunning admission, the company representative confessed to providing major gifts to a key staffer within Ross's agency, who had been a key decision-maker on the awarding of several major contracts.

The other reason for the call was to alert Ross to the fact that the staffer had made new demands for additional gifts. Things like this can land people in jail.

Ross was shaken and reached out to his CEO, Monica. She immediately set up a meeting to hear what Ross knew.

In the meeting Monica asked a few questions, mainly focused on who else was aware of the information. She then went on to compliment the employee in question but said she appreciated Ross for alerting her. She asked for time to process what she had heard.

Ross left the meeting assuming Monica would take decisive action. And she did. A few weeks later, Ross was handed a severance package and was perp-walked out the front door of the organization.

Corrupt procurement processes put organizations at risk legally, financially, and ethically, but Monica had another consideration in mind. She realized she had hired an employee who might interfere with the culture of graft in the organization. Ross did the right thing by all ethical and professional measures, but he had no idea that the corruption he uncovered was just standard practice.

When Ross was fired, he had no idea why. But then he reviewed the timeline of events and started to talk to current and former employees who explained the culture he had never studied nor understood. It was an open secret in this agency that there were benefits beyond salary and bonuses for "entrepreneurial" (corrupt) employees, but Ross knew nothing of it.

As he looked back, Ross realized he would have likely left his organization quietly and never discussed the corruption if he had known it would cost him his job. He would have never taken the job in the first place and would have left quickly if only he had known what was awaiting him.

Toxic companies that dismiss smoke detectors know that a high percentage of employees take a severance package rather than risk the potential for costly or potentially public, legal action. They play a legal game of "Chicken" with the employee, correctly assuming that few employees will pursue legal action.

EDDIE

Eddie was part of a diverse and successful accounting team in a small West Coast manufacturing company. A Latino, he enjoyed his job and coworkers but was concerned about anti-Hispanic outbursts from his Asian supervisor, Clark.

Clark's rants were inappropriate in any setting, but they even more troubling given the even demographic split between Asians and Hispanics in the department. It made things tense.

As concerns about Clark's comments hit a troubling peak, annual raises also became a concern. In this company, a pool of money was identified by senior executives and divided among the different departments. Rusty had the discretion to divide the raise funds in whichever way he chose to.

After hearing comments about pay raises from some of his Asian colleagues, Eddie was stunned. He had not gotten a raise, and after checking with all of his Hispanic colleagues, he learned that they had not received raises, either.

The raises had broken down entirely on racial lines.

Creating unnecessary conflict was not in Eddie's DNA. But with the combination of racist language and raises being distributed with such racial disparity, Eddie contacted the company's HR vice president to discuss the issue.

They met and the HR VP expressed surprise and concern. The evidence could not be explained away. He asked for time to investigate and digest the information. A few weeks later, Eddie was called back in for another meeting. The HR VP acknowledged Clark had violated company policies with his racial epithets and the troubling pattern on raises. As a result, pay would be adjusted and Clark would also be required to undergo sensitivity training.

Eddie felt good. *The system works*, he thought. And it was a good week—while it lasted.

A week after receiving the validation for his comments, Eddie was fired.

Rusty had been exposed for what he was, but Eddie had done something far worse in the eyes of management.

Despite having been on the right side of a moral and ethical issue, Eddie had shown himself as someone who would speak up if he saw a problem. As Clark was far from the only problem child in management, the company decided it would be easier to eliminate the person who pointed out problems than replaces the ones causing them.

As they say in prison, "Snitches get stitches."

MORE THOUGHTS ON WHISTLEBLOWING

The term *whistleblower* evokes a powerful image—someone standing up to expose wrongdoing in their company. And it's even powerful when you see that some companies are unwittingly bringing it on themselves. In October 2018, Amerisource Bergen (AB), a major pharmaceutical distributor, settled with federal and state governments for $625 million over allegations that the firm distributed inferior or misbranded drugs.

The whistleblower in this case was one more example of a smoke detector—someone who never intended to blow a whistle in any way to harm the company: former chief operating officer Michael Mullen. Mullen spoke up internally about his deep concern about AB's actions. When he spoke up, AB fired him. So Mullen contacted the federal government. He went from smoke detector to whistleblower. They weaponized an employee and turned him from concerned employee to government witness.

In real-life situations, you'd never be upset at the person who stops you from stepping off the curb into the path of a car. Or the friend who talks you out of getting into a bad relationship.

Yet toxic cultures cloud people's judgment more than just about any other force. In the case of Amerisource Bergen, you had a C-suite level employee pointing out the massive risk of a horrible business practice. And instead of celebrating him, they canned him—and turned a problem solver into a $625 million problem.

Leaders, recognize your smoke detectors for what they are—your best defense against sky-high legal bills and sullied reputations. They're not your enemy.

Chapter Twenty

FIREPROOFING YOUR COMPANY'S FUTURE

Some of the truly successful things we see are concepts that are not that complicated.

- In-N-Out Burger, the wildly successful fast food chain, serves only burgers, fries, and drinks.
- Chick-fil-A serves just chicken.
- WD-40 makes one spray that solves a million problems.

These three businesses are complicated in some ways, as they have multiple departments, huge staffs, and highly intricate business models. However, simplicity drives their success. They are committed to their targeted focus, don't get distracted in numerous other directions, and execute daily to sell their product. Times change and situations differ, but they always have their laser-like focus.

Fireproofing your company's future by building and protecting a good organizational culture is similar. It's takes work and time, but there's also a simplicity to it when it's successfully done and you know precisely what your focus is. When you do, the payoff is incredible.

When you analyze great organizational cultures, you see four things again and again:

1. An organization has decided what they want to be, what they believe, and what they prioritize.

2. They have decided how those values materialize in daily operations. In other words, that means projecting values internally among staff; outwardly to customers and competitors; comprehensively through ethics, safety, and operations; and globally through metrics and milestones.

3. They have committed to educating their employees on adoption of the values in a process that is not just one poster in a break room or one all-hands-on-deck speech. It infiltrates in the best of ways all that a company does in real-life examples that employees see.

4. They protect and defend their culture when necessary. That may mean defending themselves against their own employees.

In this chapter, I'll profile two long-time great cultures—Southwest Airlines and TDIndustries—that should serve as role models for every organization that wants to know how to do things right. In addition, I'll focus on two rock-star (and rock-solid) companies that have taken troubled cultures and transformed them into shining stars—Ryan LLC and Cumulus Media.

SOUTHWEST AIRLINES

At Southwest, a positive culture is palpable. It's infectious, and it touches everything the company does. If you're a customer, all you have to do is fly with them once to understand who they are.

I have been blessed to spend time over the years with Southwest executives like their late founder Herb Kelleher, their former longtime EVP and general counsel Ron Ricks, and current CEO Gary Kelly. They are all legendary—and all would agree that their biggest asset is Southwest employees. Southwest's leadership knows who they want and don't want in the hiring process. If you have a great attitude and you're willing to work, you are Southwest material. If you don't, forget it. When hired, new employees are immersed in the culture from day one, and occasionally a problem employee slips through the hiring cracks. When that happens, the employee won't last long. A good culture does not want to spoil a good thing.

Look no further than Southwest's values and mission statements to understand who Southwest is and what they believe. Their values are categorized into two groups: "Living the Warrior Way" and "Working the Southwest Way."

Living the Warrior Way includes key aspects of any good employee, namely, having a servant's heart and being fun-luving (that's no typo—spelling it luv is part of Southwest's not-too-serious a way of doing things).[1]

Working the Southwest Way means a commitment to safety and reliability and friendly customer service.[2]

Thus, what they get from their hiring process (and, ultimately, what the Southwest customer gets) is employees who work hard and humbly, are fun to be around, adhere to things that protect passengers and their coworkers, and provide excellent value.

Then, on the other job requirements, the company firmly believes and demonstrates, based on their success over the years with decades of consistent and steady profitability and a strong safety record, that they can train employees for everything else.

Finally, perhaps the most audaciously impressive sign of how successfully Southwest signals its values to employees and customers alike is by how it demonstrates what it believes in tough situations.

In *Nuts*, a book written about Southwest's culture, Herb Kelleher was quoted as saying the following: "The customer is sometimes wrong. We don't carry those sorts of [rude] customers. We write to them and say to 'Fly somebody else. Don't abuse our people.'"[3]

Employees will bend over backwards when they experience loyalty like that.

TDINDUSTRIES

TDIndustries (TD) is another company that practices what they preach in finding employees whose positive, ethical values match their outstanding culture.

TD is an employee-owned, multi-state mechanical construction and facility service company that has been recognized in *Fortune* magazine's "100 Best Places to Work" for twenty years in a row. Their revenues reached nearly $600 million in 2017. Their operations stretch across the nation.

I had the privilege of working with TD when I served as a lobbyist for a construction trade association. When I met the son of the founder and then CEO Jack Lowe Jr., President Ben Houston, and their current CEO Harold MacDowell, I met some of the finest individuals I have ever encountered in any setting—business, church, athletics, or politics. You can see the difference.

Without exception, their team is transparent, hardworking, and unceasingly positive. They serve others and lead. It's a compliment to say when you meet one TD employee, you've met them all.

TD's values are front of mind at all times, as you need look no further than the first page of their website or talk to any of their employees to find out how values are put into action.

TD's five core values are to (1) build and maintain trusting relationships, (2) fiercely protect the safety of all partners, (3) lead with a servant's heart, (4) passionately pursue excellence, and (5) celebrate the power of individual differences.[4] They then break each value down into other stated principles that further define who TD Industries is.

"Build and maintain trusting relationships" means to (1) be an empathetic listener, (2) act with fairness—no double standards, (3) speak with honesty and behave with integrity, and (4) make and keep your commitments.[5]

"Fiercely protect the safety of all partners" translates into (1) showing concern for every person, (2) "your safety is my responsibility," (3) stopping any unsafe work behaviors, and (4) zero injuries for our families.[6]

"Lead with a servant's heart" means to (1) be humble and respectful, (2) listen to understand—not to respond, (3) teach, inspire, and support others to be their best, and (4) to hold yourself and others accountable.[7]

"Passionately pursue excellence" equals (1) holding high expectations of myself and others, (2) to innovate and challenge the status quo, (3) to never stop learning, (4) and being 100-percent responsible for results—no excuses.[8]

Finally, "celebrate the power of individual differences" means (1) creating a culture of collaboration and inclusion,

(2) encouraging new ideas, (3) learning from one other's perspectives, (4) being grateful for each competitor, and (5) a commitment to achieving more together.[9]

Use ingredients like these as your foundation and expect success, long-term productivity, and integrity to follow.

RYAN LLC

Ryan LLC is a tax services and consulting firm with over 9,000 employees and seventy-five offices; it operates in forty countries. Since 1991, they have dispensed valuable information and services to their clients.

And, thankfully, years ago, Ryan employees felt empowered enough to give some valuable feedback to their founder, chairman, and CEO Brint Ryan. And he responded in precisely the way smart executives do—they listen, evaluate, and respond in ways that benefit their organizations.

From its founding in 1991, Ryan LLC was like most consulting companies: it paid well, but employees were expected to work far beyond the traditional nine to five. In fact, the minimum expectation was that employees work fifty-five hours per week in the office, plus whatever time they spent outside the office. If an employee had worked sixteen hours in one day, policies were such that the employee was expected to be in the office for eight hours the next day or risk losing time off. It was costing the company good employees by attrition and burning out many of those that remained.

Ryan was witnessing high turnover at the firm—22 percent in 2007—and decided to change his company for the better. He knew from the turnover rate, company surveys, and one-on-one feedback he received that his company had a serious problem. So he empaneled a team and worked to change the culture.

The changes that were made, called myRyan, implemented flexibility.[10] Employees have flexibility to work from home and, most importantly, are not getting the signal that they are required to be chained to a desk.

Though myRyan took time to implement and years to work out all the kinks, the results have been impressive.

Today, voluntary turnover is in the single digits, the company is regularly on the lists of *Fortune*'s "Best Companies to Work For," *Working Mother*'s "Top 100" list, "100 Best Workplaces for Women," and "100 Best Workplaces for Diversity."

And, not surprisingly, productivity and revenue rates have soared. Ryan LLC, just as they do with their clients, identified a problem and solved it. Their culture has gone from challenging to award-winning.

CUMULUS MEDIA

With its reach to 245 million people in eighty-nine US media markets and through 8,000 radio stations through its various business channels, Cumulus knows a thing or two about communications.

But when CEO Mary Berner took over the company's leadership in 2015, she learned that the company's culture was not being communicated to *anyone*. *And*, if it was being communicated, there was lots of static, but nothing that was music to people's ears.

Berner, in an October 2017 essay in *Chief Executive*, describes that her company was in "freefall" as a result of listenership declines, dropping revenue, and unsuccessful acquisitions.[11]

Just as troubling were internal factors that had nothing to do with programming: the culture was a mess. Fifty percent turnover. No employee raises in ten years. Employee surveys filled with the classic buzzwords of a troubled culture: dysfunctional, toxic, and lousy, with many employees pinning the bad corporate performance on the culture.

Just as symptomatic of the organization's problems was the disparity of life at the top and the bottom of the company food chain.

While those rank-and-file employees had gone without a raise for the previously mentioned decade, top executives were traveling via private jet and enjoying huge offices and expense accounts.

Berner knew that action was necessary and assembled her team, along with a six-step program, to fix the culture. The results have been impressive. Since 2015, the turnover rate has dropped from 50 percent to 24 percent and employee satisfaction surveys are showing positives of over 90 percent.

But it was the six-step program—that Berner refers to as a "Culture Fix Playbook"—that made all the difference.

It was focused on treating employees as valued partners in the organization's success. Berners's six steps are the following:

1. Define it. Berner describes this step as assessment of where the organization is and deciding what the company wants to be. For Cumulus, they decided that the values of "Focused, Responsible, Collaborative and Empowered" defined what they wanted to be.[12]

2. Plan it. Culture should be written out, discussed, and have its metrics evaluated regularly.[13]

3. Communicate it. Much like at TDIndustries and Southwest, great cultures talk about their values regularly. Berner went on the road and talked to employees about what the new Cumulus would be like.[14]

4. Amplify it. They looked for ways to demonstrably show that the company would be serious about its culture.[15]

5. Live it. Employees are expected to live out the company's values. If they don't, they don't last.[16]

6. Refresh it. Cumulus is looking for new and innovative ways to demonstrate their values when working with employees.[17]

And that company plane? It was sold to help pay for employee raises. What a tangible way to send a powerful message to formerly frustrated employees that the culture has truly changed.

Cumulus has gone from disconnected and distant to broadcasting its culture to employees daily. And their employees—and their revenue—have responded accordingly.

Study and learn from Southwest, TDIndustries, Ryan LLC, and Cumulus Radio, and you'll see cultural models that will elevate your organization in every possible way.

* * *

Fireproofing isn't rocket science. It's like building a great football team. You need offense and defense.

On offense, an organization needs to not only explain their values, but to live by them. When people see that values matter, people *value* them. If not, the values are not *valuable*. It's simplistic to say, but do people respect hypocrites? No. Are those who stand behind what they say usually respected by their peers? Yes.

Organizations need to tell their story and reinforce it regularly. Would you run just one commercial and expect to get results? No. When I advised political campaigns on their TV and radio advertising, it was understood that literally dozens of commercials were necessary to get a message across to voters. To instill values, organizations need to do the same.

Employees from the C-suite down; customers looking at the organization from the outside; and the media, regulators, and other stakeholders need to see values in action and adhered to.

If they don't, and a constant, steady affirmation of values is not instilled regularly, the great words that someone in HR tacked onto the bulletin board years ago will wither. Great organizations do not let that happen.

Another great play on offense is not only to adopt values but also to adapt. For instance, inclusivity was not on everyone's radar screen or priority list decades ago, but it definitely is today. A great culture will be nimble enough to adjust when situations, society, or decency demand it.

On defense, it's a matter of protecting those things that are important to the company. It's simple: don't go against your core values as a manager and require the same from employees.

The firm where I worked had no semblance of core values. It may have at some point, but other than production and revenue, the only virtue signaling I witnessed was deal cutting and self-preservation. There are leaders at companies every day who signal what's important to them. If your company is struggling with its identity, know that it's time for you to send the right kind of signals.

Chapter Twenty-One

RISING FROM THE ASHES

I'm about to mix mythology with a sitcom reference to get my point across, so get ready.

Mythology tells us about the mythical Egyptian bird—the Phoenix—that was consumed by fire and rose triumphantly from the ashes.

Not to compare myself to a mythological bird, but I know something about being burned down and coming back from it.

Breaking news to your family that you have been fired is something that leaves a mark. For me, it's as vivid today as it was when it happened. It leaves some scars, but always remember that with every scar comes a story that you're able to tell for a lifetime and occasionally share with someone who can learn from your experience.

I had to accept that I had just gone through an extraordinary experience and, after taking a couple of weeks to decompress, it was time to get focused, determine what I learned, what mistakes I made, and then get ready for the rest of my life.

As for decompression, there wasn't much of it. I went to a networking event two hours later—partly to network and partly to prove to myself that I was not going to let the firm define me.

For focus, I tuned up my resume and LinkedIn profile.

For assessment and lessons learned, it was easy. Those observations included

- I had been irrationally confident of my ability to get along with anyone, and it created a blind spot.

- Despite every sign to the contrary, I had listened to the supportive words at the beginning of the job from Cecil and Suzy and relied on that as an assurance that they would not sell me out. However, if I had watched their actions, I would have known I was a dead man. As a lobbyist, I could analyze exactly what I was witnessing—what was being said and, most importantly, what wasn't being said. But I was better watching out for others than I was in protecting myself.

- Expecting people to do the right thing in a toxic environment was unrealistic. Despite having seen numerous examples of it during my career, in toxic environments, ethics are a free-for-all and doing the right thing comes with a serious price.

- While my advocacy work was strong for protecting the interests of my clients, I had been just as weak in protecting my own. If a client had faced an issue with a competitor, I would have urged them to go on the offensive, launch a PR effort, and build a coalition to defeat the opponent, research their weaknesses, and hit back.

- I learned that a healthy culture is one of the most powerful things going in an organization. It can be the tie that binds, or it can be the hurricane that rips through a community. It's like good health—you don't always appreciate it until it's no longer there. Without it, there is weakness and a downward spiral.

And then, as I looked to move on and find my next opportunity, I learned one more thing: That is, I had a heck of a problem on my hands. The firm had become my "smelly car."

If you watched the TV show *Seinfeld*, you probably remember "The Smelly Car" episode: Jerry and Elaine go out for dinner and then to a round of parties at the homes of their friends. After arriving for dinner, they valet Jerry's car. When they finish dinner and get in the car, they realize the car reeks from the valet's body odor! They drive on to a party at a friend's house. When they arrive, they realize that not only does the car smell but they do also! The BO has permeated everything—and everyone! Elaine's boyfriend doesn't want to be near her. Even Kramer is offended by the smell. Cleaning the car does no good. Eventually, even Jerry's attempt to get rid of the car by dropping the keys in front of a thief backfired. The thief hated the smell, too!

Anything approaching a fully transparent answer left a lingering stench that would have an impact far beyond a smelly car. It would affect my ability to put food on the table.

Can you imagine telling some unsuspecting hiring manager what had occurred at the firm to spur my departure? Beginning an interview question with "Are you sitting down?" is not a great way to get hired.

This wasn't going to be easy.

Realizing that I had a problem, I sought the opinions

and insights of a hiring professional who did his best. Enter Clarence.

Clarence and I brainstormed what he believed was the perfectly packaged answer. It was decided that I should say "After achieving many great things at the firm, I decided that I wanted to move on" and smile while the interviewers gazed at me in respect and awe. It was true that I had done some good to potentially great things, but the timing of my departure was definitely not of my choosing. I figured I would be fine in giving that answer as long as no one asked me any questions beyond that point. Just like walking on a train track is safe unless there's a train coming.

Clarence's line worked extremely well—until I had to tell it to another human being.

Right out of the gate after leaving the firm, I sat in an interview with a search committee tasked with hiring for a high-profile, powerful position in Smackover, Arkansas. I had the relationships, the experience, and the skills to get this great job.

After forty-five minutes of flawless recitation of my accomplishments, my ability to lead their organization to new heights, and my name dropping of every connection I had that would undoubtedly wow them into making an offer to me on the spot, the chairman of the search committee, Chuck, said he had just one question to ask.

"Pete, I'm looking at your resume and I'm just wondering. Why aren't you working at the firm anymore?"

I was ready.

I cleared my throat, sat up straight, smiled, and delivered an answer that was not just good but also bought and paid for. After all, I had hired someone for this answer! This was a $500 response.

"Chuck, that's a great question," I said. "After achieving many great things at the firm, I decided that I wanted to move on."

Wow, that came out exactly as we practiced it! I thought.

Within seconds, I wondered if Clarence issued refunds.

"Pete, are you telling me that you just left a job for no good reason other than you wanted to walk away? You're either a quitter or a liar, and I'm not sure which," Chuck said.

The Hindenburg had a more successful trip than this trial balloon of an answer. My candidacy for the job was carried out on a stretcher that day—DOA.

The reason? No one believes that people just walk away from their jobs or, if they do, they don't respect that you walked away. They either think you're a liar or you're a quitter if you say you just left.

But if you tell people what really happened, you are bad-mouthing your employer and seen as toxic. It's a situation of rich irony and incredible frustration, and it was my new reality. I had a challenge ahead. How was I going to talk about this job to complete strangers who may want to hire me?

It's important to know exactly what you want to say when you leave an organization. You cannot and should not insult the company you left but saying nothing at all is equally problematic.

Today, when asked, I simply say that I accomplished many significant things in the role, that the job was not a long-term fit for me culturally, and that I am grateful to have served in great roles with excellent organizations. You may never find the perfect answer, and I can't claim to have one. It's one more reason to leave on your own terms.

If you've left your role and you're struggling with how to talk about your time at a toxic workplace, accentuate the positives. Instead of talking about what you didn't like about your last job, speak about what type of culture you want to be in and where you have excelled previously. By doing so, you'll have answered their question in a different way. "ABC Plumbing was a toxic cesspool where people attacked each other on an hourly basis" can become "I've succeeded in the past in working for companies with a collaborative spirit where strong relationships are built and there are positive cultures." The person you are interviewing with will understand what you're trying to say, and you'll likely have scored a few points by taking the high road.

Now, beyond the interview I referenced, life hasn't necessarily been easy since leaving the firm. Two of my favorite sayings are "God has a plan for me," and "If it doesn't kill you, it makes you stronger." Those are both impactful in my life, but trust me when I say that you don't want them both playing out in your life at the same time. However, I believe there are those times when part of life's plan is to sculpt you for something new. I've experienced some hardship and found myself at times competing for jobs that I likely would not have considered before the firm. But sometimes in life, you need to do what you need to do.

There is incredible strength that comes with adversity. Look at the power that comes through resistance training. It's literally pushing back against a force. Working out hurts, and you smell terrible after the experience, but doing it repeatedly makes you healthier, look better, and you are able to achieve more if you continue to do it.

Life's problems do the same.

Adversity can strip away arrogance and pride. It challenges the very essence of who you are. And it makes you ask very hard questions that prepare you to build up from the ashes.

I thought about writing this book for a long time, and it took years to realize what I wanted to say. I could have written a tell-all, but that would not have been productive. I could have written a simple how-to guide, but that would have been boring and tedious.

Instead, I decided to tell my story to change lives for the better. When you realize you have a story to tell that resonates in some way with virtually anyone who has ever gotten a paycheck, the ability to make an impact is incredible.

There are people today forced to deal in nearly surreal work conditions with people whose behaviors insult logic and reason and whose cultures defy most anyone's sensibilities. I'm just a guy with a strong backbone and a heck of a business network who said, "No more. Not if I can help it."

I would never compare myself to the many brave people that deal with cancer, crippling disabilities, or have been harmed in combat defending our freedoms. My experiences pale compared to their struggles and sacrifices. But adversity equips you to do some things that you never knew you could do and have some conversations you've never had, including:

- The ability to rise from the ashes. The professional challenges you face with a "firm" experience are still significant, but I'm in a unique and powerful position to make a difference for organizations across the world. Not everyone can say what I can. I'm ready to contribute my voice and my expertise in a significant way via speaking, consulting, and coaching. Of course, if you need help with your government affairs operations, I'd love to have that conversation, too.

- I have turned a challenge into an opportunity. In the coming years, I hope to speak to and work with thousands of people and organizations—to reshape cultures and improve lives. If you want to have me speak to your group or discuss ways I can be of service, contact me at www.petehavel.com or at www.arsonistintheoffice.com. Also, feel free to connect with me on LinkedIn.

- And, finally, I have the ability to not only share my story about changing cultures and protecting yourself from destructive people but also to talk to those people who may be going through difficult times. If that is you, I want you to know that not only does life get better, but that you may run into opportunities you never dreamed of. And not to preach, but to encourage when I say this: I firmly believe God has a plan for my life, and I believe this journey has shaped me to do some great things. I believe the same can happen for you.

Finally, whether you are dealing with your office's arsonist or a gaggle of hard decisions as the CEO of a company, the head of the PTA, or somebody who is at the lowest levels of the organization, let me challenge you to commit to fireproofing today.

Fireproof yourself first and foremost from people who want to burn you and your dreams down. If you're not protected, you can't do anyone else any good.

Fireproof those around you. Leaders, end the madness of continuing to let arsonists survive in your organization. I challenge you to do better—both for your own interests, as well as those of your company and your employees.

You've seen the many costs of feckless management shown in both my experience and in the anecdotes I've shared. Don't let your organization be next, because if you're not careful, it only takes one arsonist to create fires that you can't put out.

Fireproof your integrity. When arsonists burn things down, something needs to remain intact when you rebuild. Let it be your integrity and the knowledge that you are doing things that not only protect yourself but also your employees and your company's prosperity.

If your organization has a problem, own it and change it. If you need help making that change, contact me or any of the numerous people in the marketplace of ideas, who can allow you to do the important things you need to do to put out the fires, rise from the ashes, and build an incredible organization that succeeds in each and every way.

Finally, thank you to Cecil, Suzy, and Hazel. I am proof that from the worst experiences can come some of life's greatest opportunities. The wheels-off culture that I experienced for a short period of time will now be used to inspire thousands of people to do better for their organizations. It hasn't been easy for me, but what I learned and endured will benefit others by protecting good cultures and help others rise again.

Are you ready to join the fireproofing movement?

Bonus Chapter

FIREPROOFING A VOLUNTEER ORGANIZATION OR MEMBERSHIP ORGANIZATION'S CULTURE

For all of my hundreds of friends in the nonprofit world, this chapter's for you. Much like people who live charmed lives and always work in great environments, this won't affect everyone, but it will hit a lot of you at some point. That is, what do you do when dealing with a toxic membership-based organization? It's a difficult problem to navigate for staff members, but that also holds true for volunteers within the organization. I have some thoughts—some strong ones at that. When membership or volunteer organizations become toxic, they have the potential to become *extremely* toxic. And a quick fix is nearly impossible.

As I mentioned previously, I have spent a significant part of my life working inside membership organizations: Chambers of commerce and trade associations, mostly, but I have also been involved in my church, school groups, and as a volunteer for other charitable organizations. And let me tell you, arsonists are everywhere.

Volunteer organizations are the lifeblood of many communities. Chambers tie the business community together. Trade associations provide a sense of unity and focus for many businesses. Houses of worship join us together around our common faith. And school groups and charitable organizations bring us together around what motivates or inspires us to help solve a problem or better our community.

Toxic companies have been studied for years. If you pick up a copy of *Forbes* or *Inc.*, there is an excellent chance you will see a reference to some sort of corporate study, poll, or white paper on something involving culture within the business community. Some of those are referenced in this book.

More recently, numerous articles have focused on the military and its issues with toxicity. These organizations retain their employees in different ways.

Businesses offer salary, bonuses, and essential benefits like healthcare and retirement plans. These are all "handcuffs" that attach employers to employees in ways that encourage long-term commitments, even if toxicity exists. If toxicity exists, an employee can ask for a transfer to another department or look for another job. They can vote with their feet, so to speak.

The military offers salary, exceptional benefits, and a clear and noble purpose, the combination of which handcuffs service members to military service for years. Of course, it also retains employees through literal handcuffs if someone attempts to leave before their scheduled time—it's called court martial for desertion! And that's a pretty strong incentive to stick around! That doesn't necessarily solve the toxicity problem, but it definitely compartmentalizes it for the time someone serves.

As someone who has worked in non-profit volunteer organizations both as an employee (trade associations and chambers of commerce) and volunteer (churches and school organizations), I have thought a lot about what happens if your volunteer organization becomes toxic. Your organization matters to your members and volunteers, but not if they're feeling disenchanted, disenfranchised, or disgusted by the way people act at the top. The paychecks aren't keeping them there. There is no jail sentence for desertion. People can simply leave, along with their many contributions, and there is nothing to stop them. The situation—whether blatantly or subtly—can harm an organization for a long time.

What do you do?

There are three elements to consider within a volunteer organization: paid staff, rank-and-file volunteers whose involvement is less frequent and more targeted, and volunteer leadership, like members of a board of directors or committee chairs.

As for staff in a volunteer organization, if they're either the cause of the toxicity or the ones being affected by the problems, there are some tough but simple choices to consider. If a staff member is causing the toxicity, they can be terminated. If the staffer is feeling the toxicity, they can either work to help change the culture, or they can make a personal decision to leave the organization.

The rank-and-file members can affect the culture in some ways, but if they're not in leadership, they normally don't have significant power and likely do not participate as actively. Rank and file can have problem volunteers, but they'll be more the exception than the rule.

But what if neither the staff nor the rank and file is the problem?

What if the problem is at the core of the organization—the volunteer leadership or the lingering culture? The people setting the rules, being the faces of the organization, the ones modeling behavior that demonstrates what it means to be a member? What if the answer of "This is how we've always done it" prompts the organization to do culturally poisonous things? What if the culture has gone so far astray, all that is left is people who don't even know what a healthy organization looks like or you have board members in place who are happy to fill a chair, slap the board member title on a resume, and accept a free meal?

If your leadership—whether it's all of your leaders or just the most vocal ones—is toxic, you have problems you need to fix—and soon—before things get worse.

Why? It's pretty simple. Unlike employers who can negotiate with money and benefits or the military who have carrots and sticks for staying in the service, volunteer organizations offer little to tie people to their group if what the member is receiving is simply a miserable experience. Volunteers can cut off the check writing or find something better to do with their time.

It's the easiest of situations to leave: nothing is forcing someone to volunteer their time, and many people will not volunteer to be treated disrespectfully or willingly be part of something that excludes them.

There are plenty of signs to look for when considering if your organization or your leadership is toxic. If you ask many nonprofit professionals, they'll tell you that if a volunteer organization's board is toxic, the full organization likely is, as well.

What are the things to look for when considering if your volunteer organization's leadership is toxic?

- Are secret meetings commonplace? Information inside board meetings should always be confidential, but elements of the board should not be holding out on providing information to other board members. Toxic secrecy may manifest itself as board members holding secret or unofficial meetings as a group or major members of the board holding meetings on the side with a few key board allies. An executive board withholding key information from the general board can also have a debilitating effect on the discourse and trust level within an organization. When the general board does not trust the executive committee, you have the first of many problems that will emerge.

- Does information leak out? It's problematic if discussion of what's happening inside the organization is leaked shortly after the board meetings end. When this happens, board members are disrespecting their own code of conduct as board members. Leaking can be a problem in and of itself depending upon the information leaked, but it is also a major red flag.

- Are you hostage to a hostile environment? When board members do not get along, it can create a chilling effect on the ability of the board to act or respond to challenges. Do you have members resign due to run-ins with toxic leadership?

- What about personal agendas? When board members are

voting based on their own personal or political agendas, it can poison the well for ethical decision-making by all members. It lowers the standards and creates the potential of "But everyone else does it. . ." becomes an unofficial policy within the bylaws. They may also be attempting to influence on behalf of their spouse, child, or close friend.

- Are low ethical standards an issue? Those implementing the decisions of the board (the staff) must be able to trust the board. Are the decision-makers around the board room ethical people? If the answer is no, the problems will follow.

- Are meetings orderly and designed to address important business? If meetings are not solving problems, providing oversight, and shaping the strategy for the organization's future, they are likely wasting people's time.

- Are bylaws suggestions, not policies? If the board doesn't respect their own rules, who will respect them?

- Is bad behavior by board members ignored? Are there board members who are bullying other board members, launching into tirades in board meetings or other connected meetings, making self-interested deals or intimidating rank-and-file members with their behavior? If these behaviors are tolerated, your organization's future may be on life support.

- Can the full board discuss key issues? Are there segments of the board who have mentally checked out—understandably or not—from major board discussions? Whether it's because of their own lack of interest in the topics or whether they have become conditioned not to speak by overbearing members, board members at this stage are both poisoned and poison to the organization.

- Are processes and votes ethically conducted? If an organization's processes are corrupted, then the essence of being a volunteer-based membership organization is corrupt. In other words, if you hold elections for your board, for awards and other distinctions, it's important for the votes to be legitimate.

If an organization's board is toxic, there will always be spillover to the less-connected volunteers. The organization's bully—whether it's someone at a church, synagogue, chamber or PTA—does not stop with bullying just other leaders. They'll start there and likely move on to members who fit the profile that the bully is comfortable attacking.

The low ethical standards and insider dealing will become known soon enough to savvy members who wonder why their competitors who happen to be on the board appear to get most of the business from within the organization.

The leaking of business inside the organization and the ill tempers of board members will send messages loud and clear to potential volunteers and members of organizations what the group is all about.

All of these toxic behaviors lead to an important question the leadership of volunteer and membership-based organizations need to ask themselves. That is, if the organization's leadership is exhibiting these toxic behaviors, who will want to invest their time, sweat, and money into the organization if they find out what the organization is like internally?

Leadership of volunteer and membership organizations who are suffering from the traits shown earlier in this chapter need to review the check list of toxic behaviors and then take nine bold steps to bring change to the organization. A volunteer leadership retreat or orientation with an experienced facilitator can help move the discussion in the right direction. The nine ways to bring bold change to a toxic volunteer organization are the following:

1. Determine your values, lead with values, and find leaders with values that match those values. Does your organization have a values statement? A statement of what it stands for? If the organization has been operating in a toxic fashion, this step may need to wait for fresh leadership. However, creating a values statement can be an excellent prism through which to screen new leaders. Are they honest? Are they inclusive? Are they ethical? Do they work well with others? Have they served on other boards and behaved ethically and cooperatively? Can they serve in a selfless manner?

2. Make conscious decisions to avoid, where possible, bringing unethical, divisive people into leadership—This step can involve both (a) reforming how you identify and nominate leaders, and (b) keeping toxic personalities from being involved in the nomination process. Much like in the hiring process, toxic people will instinctively work to bring other toxic people into the group. Look at the system's failings and address them.

3. Choose leaders with a track record of courageous decision-making—going from toxic to transformational takes leaders who are not afraid to break some eggs, so to speak, when appropriate. Find some people who will worry about engaging in a principled debate.

4. Make bylaws matter. Ensure that your board reads, understands, and vows to uphold the bylaws—the estab-

lished, written policies of your organization. Determine if bylaws allow for removing board members and whether that process is realistic or needs to be adjusted. The past is the past and, if you're starting now, uphold the rules from this point on and gain commitment to start immediately. If you need to revise the bylaws, there's no better time than the present. Simply look to high-functioning organizations for their bylaws as a guide.

5. Address conflict-of-interest policies. End insider deals, and you'll send a clear message to your members and volunteers. Board members should sign conflict of interest forms to prohibit self-dealing, and the policy needs to be enforced

6. Be transparent. Insure that all board members receive the same information, and make sure that problems are solved as a group, not covered up.

7. Hold board members to high standards. If they are serving honorably, promote and reward board members who are serving with distinction. If they are performing poorly and creating problems that are harming the organization, create a structure to work with those board members correctively to adjust behaviors. If not, look for ways to move them into another role, or ask them to resign.

8. Make a serious effort to determine what is stopping members from wanting to discuss issues within the organization. The answer will usually center around a person or several people. Few things are more toxic than the inability to communicate.

9. Bring in leadership and consultants who know what a

successful volunteer organization looks like. Doing the same thing and expecting different results never ends well.

These nine steps may be difficult to implement in a toxic organization, but they're also necessary to take you from toxic to transformed. Good luck!

Endnotes

CHAPTER 1

1. *Cambridge Advanced Learner's Dictionary and Thesaurus,* s.v. "lobbyist," https://dictionary.cambridge.org/us/dictionary/english/lobbyist

2. "Nurses Keep Healthy Lead as Most Honest, Ethical Profession," Gallup News, December 26, 2017, https://news.gallup.com/poll/224639/nurses-keep-healthy-lead-honest-ethical-profession.aspx

CHAPTER 2

1. Movie Day at the Supreme Court or "I Know It When I See It": A History of the Definition of Obscenity, FindLaw, https://corporate.findlaw.com/litigation-disputes/movie-day-at-the-supreme-court-or-i-know-it-when-i-see-it-a.html

2. David V. Day, *The Oxford Handbook of Leadership and Organizations,* https://books.google.com/books?id=lDiTAwAAQBA-J&pg=PA266&lpg=PA266&dq=the+sustained+display+of+hostile+verbal+and+nonverbal+behaviors+tepper&source=bl&ots=Y5lHSi1kE7&sig=A-CfU3U1A15izifGSD09C7l8q7mjQgTDBEQ&hl=en&sa=X&ved=2ahUKEwj9hqO-3frfAhXni60KHT6iBIYQ6AEwBnoECAoQAQ#v=onepage&q=the%20sustained%20display%20of%20hostile%20verbal%20and%20nonverbal%20behaviors%20tepper&f=false

CHAPTER 4

1. "What You Should Know: EEOC Leads the Way in Preventing Workplace Harassment," US Equal Employment Opportunity Commission, 2018, www.eeoc.gov/eeoc/newsroom/wysk/preventing-workplace-harassment.cfm

2. Ibid.

3. Sarah Cho, "Sexual Harassment and Gender Discrimination," SurveyMonkey, Feb. 4, 2018, www.surveymonkey.com/curiosity/sexual-harassment-and-gender-discrimination-the-latest-polls-show-its-time-to-mentorher/

4. Gillian Tan and Katia Porzecanski, "Wall Street Rule for the #MeToo Era: Avoid Women at All Cost," Bloomberg, December 3, 2018, www.bloomberg.com/news/articles/2018-12-03/a-wall-street-rule-for-the-metoo-era-avoid-women-at-all-cost

5. Suzanne Lucas, "Netflix has a New Sexual Harassment Policy. It's Like 7th Grade on Steroids," *Inc.*, June 14, 2018, www.inc.com/suzanne-lucas/netflix-has-a-new-sexual-harassment-policy-its-like-7th-grade-on-steroids.html

CHAPTER 6
1. Dylan Minor and Michael Housman, "Toxic Workers," *Harvard Business Review,* October, 2015, https://dash.harvard.edu/bitstream/handle/1/23481825/16-057.pdf?sequence=1&isAllowed=y

2. Ibid.

3. Ibid.

4. Stephen Dimmock and William C. Gerken, "How One Employee Can Corrupt a Whole Team," *Harvard Business Review*, https://hbr.org/2018/03/research-how-one-bad-employee-can-corrupt-a-whole-team

5. Ibid.

6. Adam Bryant, "Walt Bettinger of Charles Schwab: You've Got to Open Up to Move Up," *New York Times*, February 4, 2016, www.nytimes.com/2016/02/07/business/walt-bettinger-of-charles-schwab-youve-got-to-open-up-to-move-up.html

CHAPTER 7
1. Jonathan Kellerman, review of *The Sociopath Next Door*, by Martha Stout, Amazon, www.amazon.com/Sociopath-Next-Martha-Stout-Ph-D-ebook/dp/B000FCJXTC

2. Martha Stout, The Sociopath Next Door (New York: Harmony, 2005), Kindle edition, www.amazon.com/Sociopath-Next-Martha-Stout-Ph-D-ebook/dp/B000FCJXTC

3. Ibid.

4. Quotes.net, STANDS4 LLC, 2019, "Hogan's Heroes, Season 1 Quotes," accessed February 7, 2019.

CHAPTER 8
1. Carol Dweck, *Mindset* (New York: Penguin Random House, 2012), as referenced by John Portch in Leaders, March 11, 2016, https://leadersinsport.com/performance/ mindset-like-muhammad-alis-john-mcenroes/

2. Susan Krauss Whitbourne, "Shedding Light on Psychology's Dark Triad," *Psychology Today,* January 26, 2013, www.psy- chologytoday.com/us/blog/fulfillment-any-age/201301/ shedding-light-psychology-s-dark-triad

3. *Encyclopedia Britannica,* s.v. "Narcissism," accessed October 2017, www.britannica.com/science/narcissism

4. Dale Hartley, "Meet the Machiavellians," *Psychology Today,* September 8, 2015, www.psychologytoday.com/us/blog/ machiavellians-gulling-the-rubes/201509/meet-the-machiavellians

5. Maria Hakki, "How to Tell Your Partner Is an Emotional Psychopath," IheartIntelligence, October 4, 2018, https://iheartintelli- gence.com/partner-emotional-psychopath/

6. *Diagnostic and Statistical Manual of Mental Disorders: (DSM-5)* (Arlington, VA: American Psychiatric Association, 2013), 92.

7. M. E. Thomas, "How to Spot a Sociopath," *Psychology Today,* May 7, 2013, last reviewed June 9, 2016, www.psychologytoday.com/us/ articles/201305/how-spot-sociopath

CHAPTER TEN
1. Patricia Hurtado, "The London Whale," Bloomberg, February 23, 2016, www.bloomberg.com/quicktake/the-london-whale

2. "The Real Cost of Absenteeism," Kaiser Permanente,
https://business.kaiserpermanente.org/insights/
the-real-cost-of-absenteeism-and-what-you-can-do-about-it

3. "Why Should You Be Concerned with Absenteeism?" Circadian
24/7 Workforce Solutions, October 14, 2014, www.circadian.com/
blog/item/43-shift-work-absenteeism-the-bottom-line-killer.html

4. "Workplace Illness and Injury Costs Employers $225.8
Billion Annually," Centers for Disease Control Foundation,
January 28, 2015, www.cdcfoundation.org/pr/2015/
worker-illness-and-injury-costs-us-employers-225-billion-annually

5. Minor and Housman, "Toxic Workers."

6. Ibid.

7. "Harassment," US Equal Employment Opportunity Commission,
www.eeoc.gov/laws/types/harassment.cfm

8. Hannah Meisel, "Illinois Jury Awards $6.45
Million to Ex-Packer Engineering Workers," Law360,
June 6, 2017, www.law360.com/articles/890420/
ill-jury-awards-6-45m-to-ex-packer-engineering-workers

9. "Supreme Court Clarifies Employer Liability for Sexual Harassment
by Supervisors," FindLaw, July 1998, https://corporate.findlaw.com/
human-resources/supreme-court-clarifies-employer-liability-for-sexu-
al-harassment.html

10. Andrew Chamberlain and Patrick Wong, "What
Matters More to Your Workforce than Money," Glassdoor,
January 18, 2017, www.glassdoor.com/research/
what-matters-more-to-your-workforce-than-money/

11. Kerri Ann Renzulli, "Workers Say They'd Give Up $21,000 a Year
for a Meaningful Job, New Survey Finds," CNBC, November 20, 2018,
www.cnbc.com/2018/11/20/workers-say-theyd-give-up-21000-a-year-
for-a-meaningful-job.html

12. "Toxic Employees in the Workplace," Cornerstone on Demand,

March 2015, www.cornerstoneondemand.com/sites/default/files/ thank-you/file-to-download/csod-wp-toxic-employees-032015_0.pdf.

13. "The Harris Poll Reputation Quotient," Harris Insights & Analytics, February 2017, https://theharrispoll.com/ reputation-quotient/

14. Heather Dinich, Adam Rittenberg, and Tom Van Haaren, "The Inside Story of a Toxic Culture at Maryland Football," ESPN, August 10, 2018, www.espn.com/college-football/story/_/id/24342005/ maryland-terrapins-football-culture-toxic-coach-dj-durkin

15. Ibid.

16. Will Felps, Eliza Byington, and Terence Mitchell, "How, When and Why Bad Apples Spoil the Barrel: Negative Group Members and Dysfunctional Groups," *Research in Organizational Behavior*, February 2007, www.researchgate.net/publication/237683988_How_ When_and_Why_Bad_Apples_Spoil_the_Barrel_Negative_Group_ Members_and_Dysfunctional_Groups

17. Alexander Tokarev, Abigail Phillips, David J. Hughes, and Paul Irwing (2017), "Leader dark traits, workplace bullying, and employee depression: Exploring mediation and the role of the dark core," *Journal of Abnormal Psychology*, 126(7), 911-920, http://dx.doi.org/10.1037/ abn0000299

18. Hara Estroff Marano, "Marriage Math," *Psychology Today*, March 16, 2004, www.psychologytoday.com/us/articles/200403/ marriage-math

19. "This Is What Negativity Does to Your Immune System, And It's Not Pretty," Quora (blog), *Forbes*, June 24, 2016, www.forbes.com/ sites/quora/2016/06/24/this-is-what-negativity-does-to-your-im- mune-system-and-its-not-pretty/#12eab6a3173b

20. Jeffrey Pfeffer, "The Enormous Toll of Toxic Workplaces," in *Dying for a Paycheck: How Modern Management Harms Employee Health and What We Can Do About It,* (New York: Harper Collins, 2018), 104.

21. BBC, "France Telecom Suicides: Prosecutor Calls for Bullying

Trial," July 7, 2016, www.bbc.com/news/world-europe-36733572

22. Marcel Schwantes, "Study: 60 Percent of Employees Are More Likely to Suffer a Heart Attack if Their Bosses Have These Traits," *Inc.*, January 2017, www.inc.com/marcel-schwantes/study-60-percent-of-employees-are-more-likely-to-s.html

23. Ibid.

24. "Workplace Bullying and Workplace Violence as Risk Factors for Cardiovascular Disease," University of Copenhagen, November 2018, *European Heart Journal*, https://academic.oup.com/eurheartj/advance-article/doi/10.1093/eurheartj/ehy683/5180493

25. Ibid.

CHAPTER ELEVEN
1. Babs Ryan, "Navigating the Minefield: Coworkers Watch Your Step," in *America's Corporate Brain Drain,* (New Rochelle, NY: Sparks Worldwide, LLC, 2008)

2. Gerald Hickson, James W. Pichert, and Steven W. Gabbe, Vanderbilt University School of Medicine, "A Complementary Approach to Promoting Professionalism: Identifying, Measuring and Addressing Unprofessional Behaviors," 2007, www.semanticscholar.org/paper/A-complementary-approach-to-promoting-identifying%2C-Hickson-Pichert/c67a19bb6d1c24aa0d3b1b88099e7f240994f136

3. Ibid.

4. Ibid.

5. Ibid.

6. Ibid.

7. Ibid.

CHAPTER THIRTEEN

1. Alexandra Berzon, Chris Kirkham, Elizabeth Bernstein, and Kate O'Keefe, "Casino Managers Enabled Steve Wynn's Alleged Misconduct for Decades, Workers Say," *The Wall Street Journal,* March 27, 2018, www.wsj.com/articles/casino-managers-enabled-wynns-alleged-misconduct-for-decades-workers-say-1522172877

2. Ibid.

3. Wikipedia, s.v. *Crawford v. Nashville,* last modified September 16, 2018, https://en.wikipedia.org/wiki/Crawford_v_Nashville

4. Lisa Rein, "FEMA Personnel Chief Harassed Women, Hired Some as Sexual Partners for Male Employees, Agency's Leader Says," *Washington Post,* July 30, 2018, www.washingtonpost.com/politics/fema-official-harassed-women-hired-some-as-possible-sexual-partners-for-male-employees-agency-chief-says/2018/07/30/964da518-9403-11e8-80e1-00e80e1fdf43_story.html?utm_term=.2834f63dd9ec

CHAPTER FIFTEEN

1. Kevin Lindsey, "Former Baylor Assistant Abar Rouse Should be Given an Opportunity," Bleacher Report, March 28, 2010, https://bleacherreport.com/articles/370071-former-baylor-assistant-abar-rouse-should-be-given-an-opportunity

2. Mike Wise, "Showtime Documentary Disgraced Resurfaces Story of Murdered Player at Baylor," The Undefeated, March 31, 2017, https://theundefeated.com/features/showtime-documentary-disgraced-resurfaces-story-of-murdered-player-at-baylor/

CHAPTER SIXTEEN

1. Lou Adler, "New Survey Reveals 85% of All Jobs Are Fillled via Networking," LinkedIn, www.linkedin.com/pulse/new-survey-reveals-85-all-jobs-filled-via-networking-lou-adler/

CHAPTER SEVENTEEN

1. "Saddam's Mouthpiece Re-emerges," CNN, June 28, 2003, www.cnn.com/2003/WORLD/meast/06/26/sprj.irq.tv.comical.ali/

2. Rob Reiner, Andrew Scheinman, and David Brown, *A Few Good Men,* United States: Castlerock Entertainment; Columbia Pictures Corporation, 1992.

3. Ibid.

CHAPTER TWENTY
1. "Southwest Citizenship," Southwest Airlines, https://www.southwest.com/citizenship/

2. Ibid.

3. Kevin Freiberg and Jackie Freiburg, *Nuts!: Southwest Airlines' Crazy Recipe for Business and Personal Success* (New York: Broadway Books, 1998).

4. TDIndustries, "Our Values," 2018, www.tdindustries.com/our-company/our-culture/

5. Ibid.

6. Ibid.

7. Ibid.

8. Ibid.

9. Ibid.

10. Lauren Dixon, "How Ryan Flipped to Flex," *Talent Economy,* December 14, 2016, https://www.clomedia.com/2016/12/14/ryan-flipped-flex/

11. Mary Berner, "How We Fixed Our Toxic Culture: The 'Culture Fix Playbook,'" *Chief Executive,* September 2017, https://chiefexecutive.net/toxic-culture/
12. Ibid.

13. Ibid.

14. Ibid.

15. Ibid.

16. Ibid.

17. Ibid.

Bibliography

Adler, Lou. "New Survey Reveals 85% of All Jobs are Fillled Via Networking." LinkedIn. www.linkedin.com/pulse/ new-survey-reveals-85-all-jobs-filled-via-networking-lou adler/

BBC. "France Telecom Suicides: Prosecutor Calls for Bullying Trial," July 7, 2016. www.bbc.com/news/world-europe-36733572

Berner, Mary. "How We Fixed Our Toxic Culture: The 'Culture Fix Playbook.'" *Chief Executive*, September 2017. https://chiefexecutive. net/toxic-culture/

Berzon, Alexandra, Chris Kirkham, Elizabeth Bernstein, and Kate O'Keefe. "Casino Managers Enabled Steve Wynn's Alleged Misconduct for Decades, Workers Say." *Wall Street Journal*, March 27, 2018. www. wsj.com/articles/casino-managers-enabled-wynns-alleged-miscon- duct-for-decades-workers-say-1522172877

Bryant, Adam. "Walt Bettinger of Charles Schwab: You've Got to Open Up to Move Up." *New York Times*, February 4, 2016. www. nytimes.com/2016/02/07/business/walt-bettinger-of-charles-schwab- youve-got-to-open-up-to-move-up.html

Centers for Disease Control Foundation. "Workplace Illness and Injury Costs Employers $225.8 Billion Annually," January 28, 2015. www.cdcfoundation.org/pr/2015/ worker-illness-and-injury-costs-us-employers-225-billion-annually

Chamberlain, Andrew, and Patrick Wong. "What Matters More to Your Workforce than Money." Glassdoor, January 18, 2017. www.glassdoor.com/research/ what-matters-more-to-your-workforce-than-money/

Cho, Sarah. "Sexual harassment and gender discrimination: the latest polls show it's time to #Mentor Her." SurveyMonkey, Feb. 4, 2018. www.surveymonkey.com/curiosity/sexual-harassment-and-gen- der-discrimination-the-latest-polls-show-its-time-to-mentorher/

Circadian 24/7 Workforce Solutions. "Why Should You Be Concerned with Absenteeism?" October 14, 2014. www.circadian.com/blog/item/43-shift-work-absenteeism-the-bottom-line-killer.html

CNN, "Saddam's Mouthpiece Re-emerges," June 28, 2003. www.cnn.com/2003/WORLD/meast/06/26/sprj.irq.tv.comical.ali/

Cornerstone on Demand. "Toxic Employees in the Workplace," March 2015. www.cornerstoneondemand.com/sites/default/files/thank-you/file-to-download/csod-wp-toxic-employees-032015_0.pdf

Day, David V. *The Oxford Handbook of Leadership and Organizations.* https://books.google.com/books?id=lDiTAwAAQBAJ&pg=PA266&lp-g=PA266&dq=the+sustained+display+of+hostile+verbal+and+nonver-bal+behaviors+tepper&source=bl&ots=Y5lHSi1kE7&sig=ACfU3U1A1 5izifGSD09C7l8q7mjQgTDBEQ&hl=en&sa=X&ved=2ahUKEwj9hqO-3frfAhXni60KHT6iBIYQ6AEwBnoECAoQAQ#v=onepage&q=the%20 sustained%20display%20of%20hostile%20verbal%20and%20nonverbal%20 behaviors%20tepper&f=false

Diagnostic and Statistical Manual of Mental Disorders: DSM-5. Arlington, VA: American Psychiatric Association, 2013.

Dimmock, Stephen, and William C. Gerken. "How One Employee Can Corrupt a Whole Team," *Harvard Business Review.* https://hbr.org/2018/03/research-how-one-bad-employee-can-corrupt-a-whole-team

Dinich, Heather, Adam Rittenberg, and Tom Van Haaren. "The Inside Story of a Toxic Culture at Maryland Football." ESPN, August 10, 2018. http://www.espn.com/college-football/story/_/id/24342005/maryland-terrapins-football-culture-toxic-coach-dj-durkin

Dixon, Lauren. "How Ryan Flipped to Flex." *Talent Economy,* December 14, 2016. www.clomedia.com/2016/12/14/ryan-flipped-flex/

Dweck, Carol. *Mindset.* New York: Penguin Random House, 2012. As referenced by John Portch in "Is your Mindset More Like Muhammad Ali's or John McEnroe's?" in *Leaders,* March 11, 2016. https://leadersinsport.com/performance/mindset-like-muham-

mad-alis-john-mcenroes/. https://leadersinsport.com/performance/
mindset-like-muhammad-alis-john-mcenroes/

Estroff Marano, Hara. "Marriage Math." *Psychology Today*, March 16, 2004. Last reviewed June 9, 2016. www.psychologytoday.com/us/afticles/200403/marriage-math

European Heart Journal. "Workplace Bullying and Workplace Violence as Risk Factors for Cardiovascular Disease." University of Copenhagen, November 2018. https://academic.oup.com/eurheartj/advance-article/doi/10.1093/eurheartj/ehy683/5180493

Felps, Will, Eliza Byington, and Terence Mitchell. "How, When and Why Bad Apples Spoil the Barrel: Negative Group Members and Dysfunctional Groups." *Research in Organizational Behavior*, February 2007. www.researchgate.net/publication/237683988_How_When_and_Why_Bad_Apples_Spoil_the_Barrel_Negative_Group_Members_and_Dysfunctional_Groups

FindLaw. "Movie Day at the Supreme Court or 'I Know It when I See It': A History of the Definition of Obscenity." https://corporate.findlaw.com/litigation-disputes/movie-day-at-the-supreme-court-or-i-know-it-when-i-see-it-a.html

_____. "Supreme Court Clarifies Employer Liability for Sexual Harassment by Supervisors," July 1998. https://corporate.findlaw.com/human-resources/supreme-court-clarifies-employer-liability-for-sexual-harassment.html

Forbes. "This is What Negativity Does to Your Immune System, And It's Not Pretty." Quora (blog), June 24, 2016. www.forbes.com/sites/quora/2016/06/24/this-is-what-negativity-does-to-your-immune-system-and-its-not-pretty/#12eab6a3173b

Freiberg, Kevin, and Jackie Freiburg. *Nuts!: Southwest Airlines' Crazy Recipe for Business and Personal Success*. New York: Broadway Books, 1998.

Gallup. "Nurses Keep Healthy Lead as Most Honest, Ethical Profession," December 26, 2017. https://news.gallup.com/poll/224639/nurses-keep-healthy-lead-honest-ethical-profession.aspx

Hakki, Maria. "How to Tell Your Partner is an Emotional Psychopath." IHeartIntelligence, October 4, 2018. https://iheartintelligence.com/partner-emotional-psychopath/

Harris Insights & Analytics. "The Harris Poll Reputation Quotient," February 2017. https://theharrispoll.com/reputation-quotient/.

Hartley, Dale. "Meet the Machiavellians." *Psychology Today*, September 8, 2015. www.psychologytoday.com/us/blog/machiavellians-gulling-the-rubes/201509/meet-the-machiavellians

Hickson, Gerald, James W. Pichert, and Steven W. Gabbe. "A Complementary Approach to Promoting Professionalism: Identifying, Measuring and Addressing Unprofessional Behaviors," Vanderbilt University School of Medicine, 2007. www.semanticscholar.org/paper/A-complementary-approach-to-promoting-identifying%2C-Hickson-Pichert/c67a19bb6d1c24aa0d3b1b88099e7f240994f136

Hurtado, Patricia. "The London Whale." Bloomberg, February 23, 2016. https://www.bloomberg.com/quicktake/the-london-whale

Kaiser Permanente. "The Real Cost of Absenteeism." https://business.kaiserpermanente.org/insights/the-real-cost-of-absenteeism-and-what-you-can-do-about-it

Kellerman, Jonathan. Review of *The Sociopath Next Door*, by Martha Stout. Amazon. https://www.amazon.com/Sociopath-Next-Martha-Stout-Ph-D-ebook/dp/B000FCJXTC

Lindsey, Kevin. "Former Baylor Assistant Abar Rouse Should Be Given an Opportunity." Bleacher Report, March 28, 2010. https://bleacherreport.com/articles/370071-former-baylor-assistant-abar-rouse-should-be-given-an-opportunity

Lucas, Suzanne. "Netflix has a New Sexual Harassment Policy. It's like 7th Grade on Steroids." *Inc.*, June 14, 2018. www.inc.com/suzanne-lucas/netflix-has-a-new-sexual-harassment-policy-its-like-7th-grade-on-steroids.html

Meisel, Hannah. "Illinois Jury Awards $6.45 Million to Ex-Packer Engineering Workers." Law360, June 6, 2017. www.law360.com/articles/890420/ ill-jury-awards-6-45m-to-ex-packer-engineering-workers

Minor, Dylan, and Michael Housman. "Toxic Workers." *Harvard Business Review,* October, 2015, 1-25. https://dash.harvard.edu/bitstream/handle/1/23481825/16-057.pdf?sequence=1&isAllowed=y

Pfeffer, Jeffrey. "The Enormous Toll of Toxic Workplaces," in *Dying for a Paycheck: How Modern Management Harms Employee Health and What We Can Do About It.* Harper Collins, March 2018.

Quotes.net, STANDS4 LLC, 2019. "Hogan's Heroes, Season 1 Quotes." Accessed February 7, 2019.

Rein, Lisa. "FEMA Personnel Chief Harassed Women, Hired Some as Sexual Partners for Male Employees, Agency's Leader Says." *Washington Post,* July 30, 2018. www.washingtonpost.com/politics/ fema-official-harassed-women-hired-some-as-possible-sexual-partners-for-male-employees-agency-chief-says/2018/07/30/964da518-9403-11e8-80e1-00e80e1fdf43_story.html?utm_term=.2834f63dd9ec

Reiner, Rob, Andrew Scheinman, and David Brown, *A Few Good Men,* United States: Castlerock Entertainment; Columbia Pictures Corporation, 1992.

Renzulli, Kerri Ann. "Workers Say They'd Give Up $21,000 a Year for a Meaningful Job, New Survey Finds." CNBC, November 20, 2018. https://www.cnbc.com/2018/11/20/workers-say-theyd-give-up-21000-a-year-for-a-meaningful-job.html

Ryan, Babs. "Navigating the Minefield: Coworkers Watch Your Step." *America's Corporate Brain Drain.* New Rochelle, NY: Sparks Worldwide, LLC, 2008.

Schwantes, Marcel. "Study: 60 Percent of Employees Are More Likely to Suffer a Heart Attack if Their Bosses Have These Traits." Inc., January 2017. www.inc.com/marcel-schwantes/study-60-percent-of-employees-are-more-likely-to-s.html

Southwest Airlines. "Southwest Citizenship." www.southwest.com/
citizenship/

Stout, Martha. *The Sociopath Next Door*. New York:
Harmony, 2005. Kindle edition. www.amazon.com/
Sociopath-Next-Martha-Stout-Ph-D-ebook/dp/B000FCJXTC

Tan, Gillian, and Katia Porzecanski. "Wall Street Rule for the #MeToo
Era: Avoid Women at All Cost." Bloomberg, December 3, 2018. www.
bloomberg.com/news/articles/2018-12-03/a-wall-street-rule-for-the-
metoo-era-avoid-women-at-all-cost

TDIndustries. "Our Values," 2018. www.tdindustries.com/
our-company/our-culture/

Thomas, M. E. "How to Spot a Sociopath." *Psychology Today*, May
7, 2013. Last reviewed June 9, 2016. www.psychologytoday.com/us/
articles/201305/how-spot-sociopath

Tokarev, Alexander, Abigail Phillips, David J. Hughes, and Paul
Irwing. "Leader dark traits, workplace bullying, and employee depres-
sion: Exploring mediation and the role of the dark core." *Journal of
Abnormal Psychology*, November 2017.

US Equal Employment Opportunity Commission. "Harassment."
www.eeoc.gov/laws/types/harassment.cfm

_____. "What You Should Know: EEOC Leads the Way in
Preventing Workplace Harassment," 2018. www.eeoc.gov/eeoc/news-
room/wysk/preventing-workplace-harassment.cfm

Whitbourne, Susan Krauss. "Shedding Light on Psychology's
Dark Triad." *Psychology Today*, January 26, 2013.
www.psychologytoday.com/us/blog/fulfillment-any-age/201301/
shedding-light-psychology-s-dark-triad

Wikipedia, s.v. *Crawford v. Nashville*, last modified September 16,
2018. https://en.wikipedia.org/wiki/Crawford_v._Nashville

Author Bio

Pete Havel has spent much of his career working for some of the nation's leading business advocacy organizations as a lobbyist and political operative, as well as serving in key roles at two strategic communications firms. He knows how to build relationships and action plans that translate into success for his clients.

He currently serves as Senior Counsel of Public Affairs for a top public relations and public affairs firm, helping clients with their government affairs needs.

In addition, Pete serves as CEO of The Cloture Group, LLC, a firm dedicated to helping organizations establish, enhance, or fix corporate cultures.

You can reach Pete at www.petehavel.com, by phone at 855-662-7766, follow him on Facebook, on Instagram at @havelpete, on Twitter at @petchavel, and on LinkedIn.

He grew up in the Boston suburb of Framingham, Massachusetts, but has called Texas home for the last thirty years. He is a graduate of Baylor University in Waco, Texas. Pete and his family live in Dallas.